Heidegger's hidd

MW01008342

In *Heidegger's Hidden Sources*, Reinhard May demonstrates that Martin Heidegger drew upon German translations of Chinese Daoist and Zen Buddhist classics for some of the major ideas of his philosophy. May also shows how Heidegger's appropriation of East Asian modes of thinking continued through conversations with Chinese and Japanese scholars over many years.

The author concentrates on a series of close textual comparisons of passages from Heidegger's major writings with excerpts from translations of Daoist classics and a collection of Zen texts – translations with which Heidegger was known to be familiar. The striking similarities in vocabulary and syntax that come to light are, May argues, too numerous to be coincidental. In addition, there is a detailed discussion of Heidegger's 'From a Conversation on Language: Between a Japanese and an Inquirer' and, published here for the first time, an English translation of the account given by the scholar with whom Heidegger had the dialogue that underlies his 'Conversation'.

Graham Parkes's complementary essay sketches a hitherto overlooked aspect of Heidegger's intellectual development by providing further details on Heidegger's contacts with several eminent philosophers from Japan, notably Kuki Shūzō, who subsequently introduced Jean-Paul Sartre to Heidegger's thought.

May's groundbreaking study will not only go a long way towards explaining Heidegger's enormous influence in Japan and China; it will also have a profound impact on future interpretations of Heidegger's work.

Reinhard May is Lecturer in the Faculty of Philosophy at the Heinrich Heine University, Düsseldorf. **Graham Parkes**, Professor of Philosophy at the University of Hawaii, is Senior Fellow at the Center for the Study of World Religions, Harvard University.

Heidegger's hidden sources

East Asian influences on his work

Reinhard May

Translated, with a complementary essay, by Graham Parkes

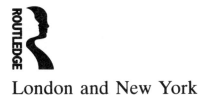

London and New York

First published 1989 in German as
Ex oriente lux: Heideggers Werk unter ostasiatischem Einfluß,
by Reinhard May, Stuttgart: Steiner Verlag Wiesbaden

English translation first published 1996
by Routledge
11 New Fetter Lane, London EC4P 4EE

Simultaneously published in the USA and Canada
by Routledge
29 West 35th Street, New York, NY 10001

Typeset in Times by Florencetype Ltd, Stoodleigh, Devon

Printed and bound in Great Britain by
Mackays of Chatham PLC, Chatham, Kent

British Library Cataloguing in Publication Data
A catalogue record for this book is available from the British Library.

Library of Congress Cataloging in Publication Data
A catalogue record for this book has been requested.

ISBN 0–415–14037–4 (hbk)
ISBN 0–415–14038–2 (pbk)

Contents

Translator's preface

The original edition of this book was published in 1989 under the title *Ex oriente lux: Heideggers Werk unter ostasiatischem Einfluss* (*Light from the East: The East Asian Influence on Heidegger's Work*).[1] While Reinhard May writes here as a philosopher, he is also a doctor of law; and the training from this background lends his treatise an air of the legal proceeding, which slowly and painstakingly adduces the appropriate evidence for the case. The case concerns the thought of Martin Heidegger and its aim of 'overcoming' the tradition of Western metaphysics, and the evidence is drawn from such a full range of Heidegger's writings that almost every published text is quoted from, along with passages from a variety of commentators. Heidegger is considered by many to be the greatest thinker of the twentieth century – a judgement that appears ever more plausible as the century draws to its end – and the charge of Dr May's treatise concerns the origins and inspiration for this thinker's thought. Through a series of painstaking textual analyses, the work argues cogently and convincingly that a major (and hitherto unacknowledged) source of Heidegger's originality is to be found in his acquaintance with East Asian philosophy.

Heidegger himself would have us believe that the origins of his thinking lie solely in the West, with the ancient Greeks and certain figures in the Judaeo-Christian tradition. From the thinkers and poets discussed in his writings, one takes the principals to be Anaximander, Heraclitus, Parmenides, Sophocles, Plato, Aristotle, Descartes, Leibniz, Kant, Hölderlin, Hegel, Schelling, Nietzsche, and Rilke. We learn also, from the occasional remark or footnote, of Heidegger's admiration for such religious or mystical thinkers as Thomas Aquinas, Meister Eckhart, and Kierkegaard. He only ever discusses one thinker from an Asian tradition (in the works published so far), the Japanese philosopher Kuki Shūzō, and then only one of his ideas, in a text from the mid-1950s that appeared in 1959.[2] The Chinese philosopher-poet Laozi (Lao Tzu) is mentioned twice, in a lecture and a journal article from the previous year. Reinhard May shows that Heidegger's interest in East Asian thought was far deeper and more important than these few mentions – and a few remarks elsewhere about 'East Asian' thinking – would suggest.[3] He does this by documenting Heidegger's familiarity with several German translations of Chinese and Japanese philosophical texts, and by showing the similarity between vocabulary and locutions in those translations and a number of key formulations of Heidegger's principal ideas – especially concerning Being (*Sein*) and Nothing (*Nichts*). The parallels are far too significant and numerous to be merely coincidental, and they become even more impressive in the context of Heidegger's close relations with a number of eminent Japanese thinkers (to be discussed below).

Heidegger's reticence with respect to Asian ideas is even more striking when seen in the light of the German philosophical tradition. Three hundred years ago Leibniz, who had a life-long interest in China, began to write about Chinese philosophy and religion, devoting special attention to the *I jing* (*Book of Changes*) and Confucianism.[4] His associate and prime correspondent, Christian Wolff, wrote on the ethical doctrines of the Chinese, with particular emphasis on Confucius.[5] Goethe, too, had a lively interest in Chinese culture, immersion in accounts of which served him as valuable recreation in times of turmoil.[6] Kant, Lichtenberg, and Herder all wrote essays on Chinese thought, and Wilhelm von Humboldt often engaged in philosophical reflection on the Chinese language.[7] With the culmination of European metaphysics in the philosophy of German idealism, with its increasingly global pretensions, Hegel and Schelling were moved to undertake studies of Chinese philosophy. With more texts available to him than to his predecessors, Schopenhauer was able to gain a somewhat better understanding of an Asian philosophy – in this instance, primarily Indian thought. With Schopenhauer we have a great Western thinker whose philosophy is informed by Asian ideas to an unprecedented extent. Following in his early mentor's footsteps, Nietzsche (on whom Heidegger published more than on any other thinker) made frequent reference to ideas from Indian philosophy and religion, and had at least a passing acquaintance with Chinese and Japanese culture.[8] It was thus quite natural for such eminent contemporaries of Heidegger's as Martin Buber, Rudolf Otto, Max Scheler, Karl Jaspers, and Karl Löwith to cultivate an interest in Asian thought and to discuss Indian, Chinese, and Japanese thinkers in their writings. In such company, Heidegger's reticence on the topic is remarkable and the grounds for it worth examining.

Heidegger's direct contact with East Asian thought dates back at least as far as 1922, when he made the acquaintance of the second most eminent figure (after Nishida Kitarō) in twentieth-century Japanese philosophy, Tanabe Hajime. He subsequently came to know personally three other major thinkers from Japan (Miki Kiyoshi, Kuki Shūzō, and Nishitani Keiji) in the course of the next fifteen years, with whom he was able to discuss East Asian thought and culture at a sophisticated level. Nevertheless, it was not until another fifteen years later, during the 1950s, that Heidegger finally brought himself to say something about East Asian ideas, stimulated apparently by a visit in 1954 from a Japanese professor of German literature, Tezuka Tomio. Dr May provides a translation of Tezuka's factual account of their conversation for comparison with a text Heidegger published in 1959, which the latter describes as having been 'occasioned' (*veranlasst*) by the visit, 'From a Conversation on Language: Between a Japanese and an Inquirer'. This dialogue of Heidegger's (one of only two he published, both in the same year) has not previously been studied in the light of his interlocutor's account of the conversation, which had been available only in Japanese.

When one reads this account, a German translation of which is included as an appendix in *Ex oriente lux*, it becomes immediately clear that Heidegger's text was 'occasioned' in only the most feeble sense by the actual conversation: for the most part, Heidegger's 'Conversation' turns out to be an imaginative reconstruction of his personal experiences over the preceding three decades with a range of Japanese colleagues, correspondence with others, readings of texts in translation, and other encounters with Japanese art and culture. As the only instance (so far) of Heidegger's discussing East Asian ideas, this work is of singular importance; and in so far as it represents an almost entirely free composition on Heidegger's part it is of even more interest. When Heidegger finally breaks his silence concerning his acquaintance with Japanese ideas, the tone and content of what he says demand close attention; and this hitherto neglected text accordingly receives an especially careful discussion in the pages below.

Another factor mentioned in the treatise that follows, the *Rezeptionsgeschichte* of Heidegger's works in East Asia, deserves mention here too, since the Eurocentrism of so much Heidegger scholarship in the West has rendered it oblivious to the long and interesting history of the reception of Heidegger's ideas in the non-Western intellectual world. It is a telling and little-known fact that the first substantive commentary on Heidegger's philosophy (aside from a few brief reviews) was published in Japan, in 1924.[9] The first book-length study of Heidegger to appear was written by a Japanese philosopher and published in 1933.[10] It is sometimes claimed – maybe correctly, though verification would be impossibly onerous – that there is more secondary literature on Heidegger published in Japanese than in any other language.[11] At any rate, Japan leads the field in translations of *Sein und Zeit*: the first Japanese version appeared in 1939 (twenty-three years before the first translation into English), and was followed by no fewer than five further translations in the subsequent three decades. (The English-reading world is still waiting for a second, improved version of *Being and Time*.)

There has often been considerable interest in Heidegger in China, though the advent of the Communist regime in 1949 occasioned a setback in Heidegger studies there.[12] There has, however, been an enormous resurgence of interest over the past decade or so: the recent Chinese translation of *Sein und Zeit* sold out of its first edition of over 50,000 copies in a few years.[13] There has always been a lively interest in Heidegger in India and Korea too;[14] and when one sees the level of enthusiasm for his philosophy in a country as far removed from Germany culturally as Thailand, the inquiring mind is bound to be stimulated.[15] Heidegger appears to be *the* modern philosopher who is most read and discussed throughout Asia, and anyone who approaches his thought equipped with an understanding of Asian philosophies will find him- or herself in startlingly familiar territory. Does there just happen to be some kind of 'pre-established harmony' between Heidegger's philosophy and Asian ideas, or are other factors at work?

The evidence from Reinhard May's textual comparisons suggests overwhelmingly that a major impetus for Heidegger's 'new beginning' (as he himself calls it) – for the trajectory of a path of thinking that is to lead beyond (or around or beneath) Western metaphysics – came from non-Western sources about which he maintained an all but complete silence. The author's undertaking is nevertheless quite in harmony with Heidegger's own method of trying to 'think what is unthought' in a thinker's works, and accords with a maxim articulated in Heidegger's 1924 lecture course on Plato's *Sophist*: 'It is in any case a dubious thing to rely on what an author himself has brought to the forefront. The important thing is rather to give attention to those things he left shrouded in silence'.[16] And to the extent that the undertaking is successful, rather than diminish Heidegger's significance as a thinker it makes him in many ways even more interesting. But it does put his achievement into perspective: in so far as his thinking has managed to 'twist free' (his own expression, with reference to Nietzsche) of the Western metaphysical tradition – and commentators like Jacques Derrida argue that this twisting free has been by no means complete – it has done so by virtue of the thinker's having one foot placed on the ground of a tradition that has been, for the most part, innocent of metaphysics (or else has become resolutely anti-metaphysical after discovering it).

Now that it can be shown that Heidegger's thinking was influenced by ideas from the East Asian philosophical tradition, a chapter of the history of modern Western ideas may have to be rewritten. There are far-reaching implications not only for how we assess Heidegger's achievement *vis-à-vis* 'the end of philosophy' and for future assessments of his place in twentieth-(and twenty-first-)century thought, but also, and especially, for comparative studies of his philosophy. Readings of the Heideggerian texts will have to be pursued from now on with what Nietzsche called 'a trans-European eye'.[17] The last few decades have seen an increasing number of studies devoted to comparisons of Heidegger's ideas with ideas from the Asian traditions. To the extent that Heidegger was familiar with German translations of some of the central texts of the Chinese Daoist and Japanese Zen traditions, comparisons with such figures as

Laozi, Zhuangzi (Chuang Tzu), Dōgen, Bashō, or Nishida – all of these potentially illuminating exercises – now have to be conducted with a somewhat different orientation.

The textual apparatus in the translation that follows is necessarily complex. Much of Reinhard May's argument depends upon close parallels between the language of passages from German translations of Chinese and Japanese texts and formulations in Heidegger's published works. That many of these early translations of Asian texts are in places inadequate, and in places inferior to the extant English translations, is beside the point – which concerns the literal content of the passages to which Heidegger had access. It is, of course, more difficult to make the argument as convincing in English, because in this case the notorious difficulty of achieving a philosophically adequate translation of Heidegger's German is compounded by the necessity to align it with English translations of German translations of East Asian texts. Obstructing the goal of keeping the aesthetic surface of the English version as clean as possible is the necessity to interpolate some of the key German terms under discussion. While readers of German would no doubt welcome more of this practice, it has been kept to a minimum in the interests of making the text as readable as possible for those unacquainted with the German language.

All references to Heidegger's texts in *Ex oriente lux* were, of course, made to the original German texts. Dr May studied all the relevant editions but gave preference to the texts as reprinted in the *Gesamtausgabe*, in which all of Heidegger's works (and lecture transcripts) are being reissued with his own comments, a minimal textual apparatus, and editorial emendations that are claimed to be definitive. Given the exorbitant cost of reacquiring Heidegger's works in the *Gesamtausgabe* editions, all but the wealthiest scholars find it more practicable to continue to work with the earlier standard editions of the works published by Klostermann, Neske, and Niemeyer. Since the pagination of these texts is given in the *Gesamtausgabe* versions, it will be to these more accessible standard editions that references in the notes will be made, even though in all cases the relevant passages have been checked against the texts reprinted in the *Gesamtausgabe*.

In order to distinguish the author's notes from the translator's, the former are printed as footnotes and the latter as endnotes at the end of the main text. In referring to works of Heidegger's that have been translated into English, the English edition will be cited in the footnote, while references to the German original will generally be relegated to the endnotes. The English translations have been made in all cases from Heidegger's original German and often differ from the extant English renderings of the passages in question. References to works that have not been translated are retained in the footnotes. A similar policy has been adopted in the case of the secondary literature referred to in the main text, most of which is in German. In cases where the works are available in English translation, these have been cited (with the translation modified where appropriate) in the footnotes and the German originals in the endnotes.

The bulk of the texts discussed by Reinhard May dates from the period after the Second World War, though he also adduces some important passages from earlier works. A conversation with Nishitani Keiji (not long before his death in 1990) in which he spoke of his talks with Heidegger during the late 1930s, prompted me to inquire into the possible influences from Japanese philosophy on the pre-War development of Heidegger's thought. The focus on an earlier period and an approach from a somewhat different angle bring to light, it seems to me, a number of considerations that finely complement Dr May's conclusions. He has graciously consented to have my essay on this topic published together with the translation of *Ex oriente lux*. I am grateful to him also for his most helpful collaboration on the translation project.

NOTES

1   This original edition was dedicated to Maehara Shigenobu.
2   Japanese and Chinese names are given in the East Asian order: family name first, followed by the given name(s) – unless cited as authors of works in a Western language.
3   For a discussion of the half-dozen texts in which reference is made to things East Asian, see Chapter 1 below.
4   See *Gottfried Wilhelm Leibniz: Writings on China*, translated by Daniel J. Cook and Henry Rosemont, Jr (Chicago 1994), which contains translations of his 'Preface to the *Novissima Sinica*' (1697/99), 'On the Civil Cult of Confucius' (1700), 'Remarks on Chinese Rites and Religion' (1708), and 'Discourse on the Natural Theology of the Chinese' (1716), as well as an informative introduction that emphasizes the generally unappreciated extent of Leibniz's interest in and knowledge of Chinese thought. See also David E. Mungello, *Leibniz and Confucianism: The Search for Accord* (Honolulu 1977).
5   Christian Wolff, 'Rede von der Sittenlehre der Chineser', in *Gesammelte Werke: Kleine philosophische Schriften* (Halle 1740), 6:17–296; reprinted in Adrian Hsia, ed., *Deutsche Denker über China* (Frankfurt 1985), 42–72 (which also contains Leibniz's foreword to *Novissima Sinica*). For a good selection of secondary literature, see Julia Ching and Willard G. Oxtoby, eds, *Discovering China: European Interpretations in the Enlightenment* (Rochester [NY] 1992).
6   In a letter from 1813, Goethe wrote: 'I have made an especially thorough study of *China* and all that belongs to it. I had, as it were, preserved this important land and set it apart, so that in case of emergency, as now, I can take refuge there. To find oneself in completely new circumstances, if only in thought, is very salutary' (Letter of 10 November 1813, to K. L. von Knebel, in *Goethes Briefe: Hamburger Ausgabe* [1965], 3:245).
7   See the texts by Kant, Lichtenberg, Herder, Hegel, and Schelling (as well as by Buber and Jaspers) anthologized in Hsia, *Deutsche Denker über China*. See von Humboldt's essays, 'Lettre à Monsieur Abel-Rémusat sur la nature des formes grammaticales en général et sur le génie de la langue chinoise en

particulier' (1825–6) and 'Uber den grammatischen Bau der chinesischen Sprache' (1826), in the *Akademie-Ausgabe* of the *Werke*, vol. 5: 254–324. The same author makes frequent reference to Chinese in *On Language: The Diversity of Human Language-Structure and its Influence on the Mental Development of Mankind*, translated by Peter Heath (Cambridge 1988) – a translation of his *Über die Verschiedenheit des menschlichen Sprachbaus und ihren Einfluss auf die geistige Entwickelung des Menschengeschlechts* (1836), which is referred to on several occasions below.

8 On this topic, see Graham Parkes, ed., *Nietzsche and Asian Thought* (Chicago 1991), and also 'Nietzsche and East Asian Thought: Influences, Impacts, and Resonances', in Kathleen Higgins and Bernd Magnus, eds, *The Cambridge Companion to Nietzsche* (Cambridge 1995), 356–83.

9 Tanabe Hajime, 'Genshōgaku ni okeru atarashiki tenkō: Haideggā no sei no genshōgaku' ('A New Turn in Phenomenology: Heidegger's Phenomenology of Life'), *Shisō* (Tokyo), October 1924; reprinted in *Tanabe Hajime zenshū* (*Collected Works of Tanabe Hajime*), vol. 4: 17–34. A German translation of this essay is available in Hartmut Buchner, ed., *Japan und Heidegger* (Sigmaringen 1989), 89–108. Subsequent references to this volume – an invaluable source on the relations between Heidegger and Japanese philosophers – will be abbreviated as '*JH*'.

10 Kuki Shūzō, *Haideggā no tetsugaku* (*The Philosophy of Heidegger*) (Tokyo 1933).

11 For a partial listing of the literature in Japanese, see Hans-Martin Sass, *Martin Heidegger: Bibliography and Glossary* (Bowling Green 1982).

12 Not long ago, I asked an eminent Chinese scholar of Heidegger in Beijing about the vicissitudes of teaching Heidegger's philosophy in Chinese universities. Had he been able to teach Heidegger continuously over the past several decades? 'Yes', was the answer; 'but after the "liberation" of the country in 1949, things were at first very difficult, and one could only teach Heidegger's works *mit Kritik*' (!). Nowadays, apparently, the criticism is optional.

13 While various sections of *Being and Time* had been translated before, the first complete translation into Chinese, *Cun zai yu shi jian*, by Chen Jiaying and Wang Qingjie under the supervision of Professor Hsiung Wei (who had studied with Heidegger in Freiburg in the 1930s), was published in Beijing in 1987. A second edition was published in Taiwan in 1990.

14 On the reception of Heidegger's ideas in Korea, see Gwang-Il Seo, *Die Heidegger-Rezeption in Korea. Mit einem Einblick in die Probleme der Heidegger-Forschung und Interpretation* (Dissertation, Heinrich Heine University, Düsseldorf, 1990/1).

15 For a variety of essays on Heidegger in relation to non-Western philosophies, see Graham Parkes, ed., *Heidegger and Asian Thought* (Honolulu 1987). Subsequent references to this volume will be abbreviated as '*HAT*'.

16 Heidegger, *Gesamtausgabe*, 19:46. The passage is quoted as the epigraph to Jacques Taminiaux, *Heidegger and the Project of Fundamental Ontology*, translated by Michael Gendre (Albany 1991), a book that discusses Heidegger's silence with respect to sources of his early thought in texts by such thinkers as Aristotle, Hegel, and Nietzsche.

17 See Nietzsche's letter to Paul Deussen (3 January 1888) in which he writes that his 'trans-European eye' lets him see that 'Indian philosophy is the only major parallel to our European philosophy'.

Abbreviations

WORKS BY HEIDEGGER

English translations

DT	*Discourse on Thinking*
EGT	*Early Greek Thinking*
ID	*Identity and Difference*
IM	*An Introduction to Metaphysics*
PLT	*Poetry, Language and Thought*
QB	*The Question of Being*
QT	*The Question of Technology*
TB	*On Time and Being*
WCT?	*What is Called Thinking?*
WL	*On the Way to Language*
'WM?'	*'What Is Metaphysics?'*
WT?	*What is a Thing?*

German texts

FD	*Die Frage nach dem Ding*
G	*Gelassenheit*
GA	*Martin Heidegger: Gesamtausgabe*
Hw	*Holzwege*
SD	*Zur Sache des Denkens*
'SLT'	*'Seminar in Le Thor (1969)'*
SZ	*Sein und Zeit*
US	*Unterwegs zur Sprache*
VA	*Vorträge und Aufsätze*
Wm	*Wegmarken*

Other works

EMH	*Erinnerung an Martin Heidegger*
HAT	*Heidegger and Asian Thought*
JH	*Japan und Heidegger*
P	Petzet, *Encounters and Dialogues with Martin Heidegger*
PEW	*Philosophy East and West*

Introduction

1 The following investigation is a contribution to Heidegger scholarship that involves a certain amount of daring. For it engages, from a transcultural perspective, certain complex information, hardly broached until now, concerning the hidden sources of his thought. It thereby engages the frequently remarked strangeness of Heidegger's late work. At the same time the investigation is to be understood as a contribution to the discipline of comparative philosophy.

   The primary concern is not with an interpretation but rather with a presentation and documentation of the central ideas and key terms of Heidegger's thinking in the light of the basic ideas of Daoism and, where appropriate, of Zen Buddhism. This procedure is called for by the task that has been undertaken here, and to that extent the customary work of interpretation has been relegated to the background.

2 In view of the numerous and widely dispersed indications of particular relations between Heidegger and East Asia, the investigation proceeds from the hypothesis that his work was influenced by East Asian thought to a hitherto unrecognized extent (see Chapter 1). It begins by comparing Heidegger's text, 'From a Conversation on Language', with a report by the renowned Japanese Germanist Tezuka Tomio, who had a conversation with Heidegger in 1954 to which the text refers (Chapters 2 and 7).* This conversation provides some valuable clues concerning the question of influence.

---

* Translator's Note. Names are given in the East Asian order, family name followed by given name(s), except where cited as authors of texts published in a Western language. The original title of Heidegger's text, 'Aus einem Gespräch von der Sprache – Zwischen einem Japaner und einem Fragenden', has been rendered more literally here than in the English translation by Peter D. Hertz, 'A Dialogue on Language'. The former is to be found in *Unterwegs zur Sprache* (Pfullingen 1959), 83–155; henceforth abbreviated as '*US*' (the page numbers of this edition are given in the version reprinted in the *Gesamtausgabe*, vol. 12), and the latter in *On the Way to Language* (New York 1971), 1–54; henceforth '*WL*'. Heidegger's 'From a Conversation' gives a greater impression of the work's deriving from an actual conversation than does 'A Dialogue', which suggests a freer, more literary composition; for the importance of this distinction, see Chapter 2 below. [Subsequent notes by the translator will be marked by letters and found at the end of the main text, while short interpolations into the original notes will be enclosed in brackets.]

Through a partial exegesis of representative Heideggerian texts, two subsequent chapters (3 and 4) consider Heidegger's own self-interpretations in order to try to discover his *main thought* by way of his own guiding principles and key terms. Thus careful attention is paid to his sentence-construction, choice of words, and the essential word-fields he creates (excluding fillers and flourishes), since this opens up the possibility of decoding and making clear what is really meant (and thought). In the course of exhibiting the main thought, further significant thoughts are brought to light which also condition the meaning and aim of his thinking. Through comparisons with relevant passages from German translations of East Asian classics the corresponding sources of this thinking will eventually be clarified.

Chapter 5, leading up to the conclusions in the next chapter, attempts to show that Heidegger himself, in indicating his *new* path of thinking, makes a pertinent 'confession' in *his own* way.

3 The investigation concludes that Heidegger's work was significantly influenced by East Asian sources. It can be shown, moreover, that in particular instances Heidegger even appropriated wholesale and almost verbatim major ideas from the German translations of Daoist and Zen Buddhist classics. This clandestine textual appropriation of non-Western spirituality, the extent of which has gone undiscovered for so long, seems quite unparalleled, with far-reaching implications for our future interpretation of Heidegger's work.

1   Indications

But if human language is in the word, only then is it in order. If it is in order, there is a chance of access to the *hidden sources*.[a]

Martin Heidegger

1   We are indebted to Chang Chung-yuan,[1] Paul Shih-yi Hsiao,[2] Tezuka Tomio,[3] Hans A. Fischer-Barnicol,[4] and Heinrich Wiegand Petzet,[5b] as well as to others among Heidegger's contemporaries for manifold indications of his interest in East Asian thought, and in Daoism and Zen Buddhism especially. We are also informed about Heidegger's numerous contacts with the East Asian world, with a world to which, according to Petzet, he felt himself drawn and 'which gladly accepted him' (P 166/175f). Neither Heidegger's interest nor his contacts have been contested; moreover, Petzet remarks that Heidegger was also familiar with East Asian thinking.[6] Heidegger himself draws our attention to his acquaintance with this topic, in so far as he speaks *directly*, in several passages in works from the 1950s that have been published, about 'East

---

[1] Chang Chung-yuan, 'Reflections', in G. Neske, ed., *Erinnerung an Martin Heidegger* (Pfullingen 1977), 65–70 [this volume abbreviated in subsequent references as '*EMH*']; 'The Philosophy of Taoism according to Chuang Tzu', *Philosophy East and West* 27 (1977): 409–22 [henceforth '*PEW*'].
[2] Paul Shih-yi Hsiao, 'Wir trafen uns am Holzmarktplatz', in *EMH* 119–29; 'Heidegger and Our Translation of the *Tao Te Ching*', in *HAT* 93–101.
[3] Tezuka Tomio, 'Haidegga to no ichi jikan' ('An Hour with Heidegger'), in 'Kotoba ni tsuite no taiwa' ('From a Conversation on Language'), *Haidegga zenshū* (*Complete works of Heidegger*) 21 (Tokyo 1968; 3rd edition: 1975), 159–66; see the translation of this essay in Chapter 7, below. We are also indebted to another Japanese contemporary of Heidegger's, Nishitani Keiji, for valuable information about Heidegger's interest in Zen Buddhism, and in particular about his reading of the volume by Ohazama Shūei, *Zen: Der lebendige Buddhismus in Japan*, edited by August Faust (Gotha/Stuttgart 1925). See the account by Graham Parkes, in *HAT* 9f.
[4] Hans A. Fischer-Barnicol, 'Spiegelungen – Vermittlungen', in *EMH* 87–103.
[5] Heinrich Wiegand Petzet, *Encounters and Dialogues with Martin Heidegger, 1929–1976*, translated by Parvis Emad and Kenneth Maly (Chicago 1993), 73, 166–83, 217 [future references will be made simply by the abbreviation 'P' followed by the page numbers of the English and German editions respectively]; 'Die Bremer Freunde', in *EMH* 179–90.
[6] P 169, 18, 59/175–8, 24, 65.

Asian language', the notion of *dao*, and Laozi (Lao Tzu).[7c] All this is known well enough.

Less well known are two further references to Laozi. First, we learn from Petzet that Heidegger quoted a large part of Jan Ulenbrook's translation of Chapter 47 of the *Laozi* in a letter to Ernst Jünger (P 182/191). Petzet does not, however, note that Heidegger departs from Ulenbrook's translation[8] in the fourth line of his citation and apparently gives his own version at this point: instead of Ulenbrook's 'seeing the way of heaven' he writes 'seeing the whole of heaven', thereby eliminating the word 'way' (*dao*). The rendition is thus in part an Ulenbrook-Heidegger version. Second, there is a similar instance in Heidegger's letter to Hsiao of 9 October 1947 (reproduced in *HAT* 102). Here Heidegger paraphrases Hsiao's translation of Chapter 15 of the *Laozi*, which runs:

> Who is able to make still and gradually clarify what is muddy?
> Who is able to move and gradually animate what is at rest?
>   (*EMH* 127)[d]

At Heidegger's request, Hsiao had earlier made a calligraphy of these lines for him.

> I inscribed these two lines of eight characters each on such parchment as was then available; 'the *dao* of heaven', which is not in the text, I wrote as a decorative device in the middle. I gave a careful etymological explanation of all the characters, so that he could grasp everything in detail. The Heideggerian version again shows the depths of his thinking (*HAT* 100).

In his letter to Hsiao, Heidegger performs the following two variations of his own:

> Who is able to be still and from and through stillness put something on the way (move it) such that it comes to light?[e]

While this version, which Heidegger puts in quotation marks, is apparently a product of the collaboration between Heidegger and Hsiao (guided by the latter's competence in sinology), the version that immediately follows in the letter can be ascribed to Heidegger alone. In his own handwriting it reads:

---

[7] Martin Heidegger, *The Question of Being*, translated by William Kluback and Jean T. Wilde (New York 1958), 107 [henceforth '*QB*']; *Identity and Difference*, translated by Joan Stambaugh (New York 1969), 36 ['*ID*']; 'The Nature of Language', in *WL* 57–108, 92; 'Grundsätze des Denkens', in *Jahrbuch für Psychologie und Psychotherapie* 6 (1958), 33–41, 40. See also the various remarks in 'From a Conversation on Language' (to be discussed in Chapters 2 and 5 below), and in 'Science and Reflection', in *The Question Concerning Technology and Other Essays*, translated by William Lovitt (New York 1977), 155–82, 158.
[8] *Lao Tse: Tao Te King. Das Buch vom rechten Wege und von der rechten Gesinnung*, translated by Jan Ulenbrook (Frankfurt 1980), 147.

Who is able by making tranquil to bring something into Being?
The *dao* of heaven.[f]

Three further chapters from the *Laozi* (18, 76, and 7) that are brought into the conversation (as communicated by Hsiao) shed further light on Heidegger's acquaintance with this text. Hsiao also reports his saying, in his lecture on culture and technology:

> one would have to see old things with a newer, farther look. If we were to attempt, for example, to 'ground' God through the traditional proofs of His existence – the ontological, cosmological, or teleological – we would then diminish God, who is more, and ineffable 'like the *dao*' (*EMH* 127).

Further indications can be drawn from Petzet's accounts. For example:

> In the conversation [1950] about the 'fourfold' we touched on the topic of Laozi, to which a young woman made an essential contribution. In the end the guests ... had perhaps sensed something about that 'turn' that ... could eventuate in a memorial thinking. The meeting with Heidegger thus became for many participants a sign (P 73/80).

Finally, Petzet draws our attention to two other informative remarks of Heidegger's. First, in conversation with a Buddhist monk from Bangkok in September 1964, Heidegger said that 'he himself would often hold to Laozi – but that he knew him only through the German intermediaries, such as Richard Wilhelm'.[9] Second, Petzet reports that on hearing the Buddhist monk say that 'nothingness is not "nothing", but rather the completely other: fullness. No one can name it. But it – nothing and every-thing – is fulfillment', Heidegger responded with the words, 'That is what I have been saying, my whole life long' (P 180/190). Heidegger apparently said something similar in connection with one of D. T. Suzuki's books.[10] We learn from Petzet again that Heidegger was familiar as early as 1930 with a German version of the *Zhuangzi (Chuang Tzu)*, a selection edited

---

[9] P 174/183. In addition to the 1911 translation of the *Laozi* by Richard Wilhelm, Heidegger was no doubt also quite familiar with the version by Victor von Strauss from 1870 (see bibli-ography), since he cites this translation of *Laozi* 28 in his essay 'Grundsätze des Denkens' (though the citation ought to read Chapter XXVIII rather than Chapter XVIII). He must also have been familiar with Hsiao's translation of the *Laozi* into Italian: *Il Tao-te-King di Laotse: Traduzione dal testo critico Cinese*, translated by Paolo Siao Sci-Yi (Bari 1941, 1947), since Hsiao presented him with a copy in 1942 (see *EMH* 121). (Heidegger apparently read Italian fluently.)

The conversation between Heidegger and the monk from Bangkok, Bikkhu Maha Mani, took place on Southwest Television in Baden-Baden on 28 September 1964; a previous conversation between the two, lasting several hours, had taken place at Heidegger's home in Freiburg (P 170/179).

[10] William Barrett, 'Zen for the West', introduction to D. T. Suzuki, *Zen Buddhism* (Garden City, NY 1956), xi: 'A German friend of Heidegger told me that one day when he visited Heidegger he found him reading one of Suzuki's books. "If I understand this man correctly," Heidegger remarked, "this is what I have been trying to say in all my writings".'

by Martin Buber. This edition, a slim volume of 124 pages and the first German book edition of the *Zhuangzi*, was published in 1910 by Insel Verlag in Leipzig under the title *Speeches and Parables of Tschuang-Tse*.[11g] Heidegger responded to a certain issue by quoting and interpreting a passage half a page long entitled 'The Joy of the Fishes'.[12] Thirty years later Heidegger once again deals publicly with a passage from Buber's edition of the *Zhuangzi*, the one-page episode entitled 'The Chimes-Stand'.[13] And on the occasion of a visit from Chang Chung-yuan in Freiburg in 1972, Heidegger showed his guest, according to the latter's report, a German translation of the *Zhuangzi* and posed a number of questions which they then discussed (*PEW* 27:419).

It is clear from all this that Heidegger valued and appreciated East Asian thought, and Daoist ideas above all. Nor, obviously, was there a dearth of relevant information available, which he could easily have gleaned from the literature in German and English. Heidegger received numerous visits from East Asian colleagues over a period of about fifty years, and in the course of conversations with them he apparently listened with patient attention to the responses they would give to his precisely formulated and penetrating questions.[14] Hsiao's report, in particular, underscores this assumption (*EMH* 126f). Just how well Heidegger was actually acquainted with Daoist ideas can only be surmised at this point, and so we shall leave this question aside.[15]

2.1 Heidegger's thinking definitely exhibits not insignificant similarities with East Asian thought. An indication of this comes, again, from Hsiao, who writes as follows: 'Much of what [Heidegger] has "brought to language" has ... been said often in the same or a similar way in the

---

[11] *Reden und Gleichnisse des Tschuang-Tse*. Deutsche Auswahl von Martin Buber (Leipzig 1910). This selection edited by Buber first appeared two years before the nearly complete German translation by Richard Wilhelm (1912), and was followed by subsequent editions in 1918, 1920, 1921, 1922 (Parkes erroneously takes the 1921 edition to have been the first [*HAT* 138–9]). Buber's afterword to his selection is reprinted in Martin Buber, *Werke 1: Schriften zur Philosophie* (Munich 1962), 1021–51, as well as in Adrian Hsia, ed., *Deutsche Denker über China* (Frankfurt 1985), 282–318. New editions (partly revised) of the selections from the *Zhuangzi* appeared in Zürich (1951 – with an interesting foreword by Buber to the effect that the volume had been forgotten since the beginning of the Hitler era), and also in Frankfurt (1976, 1981 – with the first four chapters of the afterword abridged, and 1990).

[12] P 18/24. The passage comes from Chapter 17 of the *Zhuangzi* [English translation of Buber's text: *Chinese Tales*, 59].

[13] P 59, 169/65, 178. To judge from the heading, this could only be taken from the Buber edition; the passage is from Chapter 19 of the original text [*Chinese Tales*, 67].

[14] See P 166/175ff; Chang Chung-yuan (*PEW* 27:419); and Tezuka (note 4 above) – to name only these two as representative of many other Chinese and Japanese interlocutors, and not forgetting Kuki Shūzō (see Chapter 2) from the earlier period and Hsiao from the later.

[15] This question will presumably claim our heightened attention at some later date. For the time being we can let it rest and regard our present state of knowledge as sufficient for the purpose in question.

thinking of the Far East'.[16] While these kinds of considerations are gradually coming to the attention of Heidegger studies in Europe, they are rarely given further discussion. Nor has there been much response to the astonishing fact that the reception of his thought in Japan has been for over sixty years as thorough as it has been comprehensive – a fact that can and should be taken as importantly indicative of Heidegger's relations to East Asian thought.

By comparison with the enormous amount of secondary literature on Heidegger, comparative philosophical studies in Western languages play only a very minor role even though they are sometimes of high quality, as evidenced by the 1987 volume *Heidegger and Asian Thought* edited by Graham Parkes. Heidegger himself did not fail to acknowledge such attempts to show correspondences[17] and agreement[18] between a thinking that *overcomes metaphysics* and an East Asian philosophical tradition that lacks metaphysics[19] in the Western sense.[20] And yet, while on the one hand he treated such attempts with a certain scepticism,[21] on the other, as Otto Pöggeler has written (*HAT* 49), he 'gladly acknowledged to visitors the closeness of his thinking to the Taoist tradition and Zen Buddhism'.

[16] Hsiao, *EMH* 120. See also Kah Kyung Cho, *Bewusstsein und Natursein: Phänomenologischer West-Ost-Diwan* (Freiburg/Munich 1987), 88–103. (The third chapter of this book was previously published as 'Gedanken abseits der dichotomischen Welterklärung', in *Natur und Geschichte: Karl Löwith zum 70. Geburtstag* [Stuttgart 1967], see 74ff) For an earlier acknowledgement of Cho's stimulating discussion, see Reinhard May, *Frieden und die Aufgabe des Rechts* (Wiesbaden 1979), 152.

[17] From the imposing amount of literature dealing comparatively with correspondences or similarities between Heidegger's thinking and East Asian thought, the following are worthy of mention (in chronological order): Carl T. Smith, 'A Heideggerian Interpretation of the Way of Lao Tzu', in *Ching Feng* 10 (1967):5–19, esp. 11–15; Elisabeth Feist Hirsch, 'Martin Heidegger and the East', in *PEW* 20 (1970):247–263, esp. 251–6; Chang Chung-yuan, *Tao: A New Way of Thinking – A Translation of the Tao Te Ching with an Introduction and Commentaries* (New York 1975), esp. vii–xxviii; Kōichi Tsujimura, 'Die Seinsfrage und das absolute Nichts-Erwachen – In memoriam Martin Heidegger', in *Transzendenz und Immanenz* (Stuttgart 1977), 289–301, esp. 293ff, and 'Martin Heidegger im Zeugnis von Kōichi Tsujimura', in Richard Wisser, ed., *Martin Heidegger im Gespräch* (Freiburg/Munich 1970), 27–30, 27; Cheng Chung-Ying, 'Remarks on the Ontological and Transontological Foundations of Language', in *Journal of Chinese Studies* 5 (1978):335–40, esp. 337, 339; Shizuteru Ueda, 'Die zen-buddhistische Erfahrung des Wahr-Schönen', in *Eranos Jahrbuch* 53 (1984):197–240, esp. 209–16; Hans-Peter Hempel, *Heidegger und Zen* (Frankfurt a.M. 1987), esp. 21–5, 138ff, 160ff.

[18] See, for instance, Hwa Yol Jung, 'Heidegger's Way with Sinitic Thinking', in *HAT* 217–44, esp. 218, 231–7.

[19] Joan Stambaugh, 'Heidegger, Taoism and the Question of Metaphysics', in *Journal of Chinese Philosophy* 11 (1984):337–52, 348, 350 (reprinted in *HAT* 79–91, 88, 90). See also Cho, *Bewusstsein und Natursein*, 88–103.

[20] See the English translation of Heidegger's letter to the participants in the 'Conference on Heidegger and Eastern Thought' held in Honolulu from 17 to 21 November 1969, reprinted by W. E. Nagley in *PEW* 20 (1970):221.

[21] As Heidegger writes in the letter cited in the previous note: 'The greatest difficulty in this enterprise always lies, as far as I can see, in the fact that with few exceptions there is no command of the Eastern languages either in Europe or the United States'. Compare P 176/185.

2.2   Considering all the indications adduced above, it is reasonable to ask whether the manifest correspondences and similarities are simply a matter of chance, or whether, put pointedly, they were deliberately elaborated by Heidegger and thus represent the unrecognized or merely unacknowledged result of a reception and integration of East Asian thought on his part. It is in any case no longer possible peremptorily to dismiss the carefully formulated question of the influence of East Asian thought on Heidegger, especially since Hsiao remarks that the collaboration on a partial translation of the *Laozi* (undertaken at Heidegger's request!) had some influence on him.[22]

Hsiao has reported at some length on his 1946 collaboration with Heidegger in two closely concurrent versions, the first of which appeared only in 1977, a year after Heidegger's death, when it elicited considerable astonishment.[23] Since Hsiao's account is readily available and may be well known, there is no need for a lengthy recapitulation here. Both reports make clear (the second was written specially for the Parkes volume in 1987) that the eight chapters of the *Laozi* that they worked on translating 'exercised some influence' on Heidegger (*EMH* 127). Unfortunately, even if one restricts consideration to the chapters on *dao*, one can only speculate about which of these they may have worked on.[24] Collaboration on the project was not resumed after the summer of 1946. According to Fischer-Barnicol, Heidegger attempted to produce with Hsiao a German version of the *Laozi* 'and abandoned it after eight chapters'.[25] Their extremely thorough attempts at translation were based, according to Hsiao, on the version of the original text edited and with a commentary by Zhiang Xi-zhang.[26] Heidegger did not give Hsiao any of the texts of their tentative translations, and it is questionable whether they still exist. According to Pöggeler (*HAT* 77), they have not yet been found in Heidegger's *Nachlass*.

In this context the following remark by Chang Chung-yuan deserves particular attention: 'Heidegger is the only Western philosopher who not only thoroughly intellectually understands but has intuitively grasped Taoist thought'.[27] Even if one is dubious about Chang's assessment, which

---

[22] Hsiao, *EMH* 127; also *HAT* 93, 98.

[23] Significant here is Petzet's saying that even he, as a close friend of Heidegger's (as his book on him makes abundantly clear), learned of the translation project only after Heidegger's death (P 181/191); but compare Fischer-Barnicol's report (*EMH* 102). Many considerations point towards the fact that Heidegger's '*Laozi* project' (and this seems to be true of his engagement with Daoist ideas in general) was to be undertaken 'in strictest secrecy' [*strikt privatissime*] (see Cho, *Bewusstsein und Natursein* 90).

[24] The relevant chapters of the *Laozi* would be 1, 15, 18, 25, 32, 37, 40, and 41. Compare Paul Shih-yi Hsiao, 'Laotse und die Technik', in *Die Katholischen Missionen* 75 (1956):72–4.

[25] According to a communication of Heidegger's reported by Fischer-Barnicol (*EMH* 102). Compare Hsiao's account: 'He pointed his index finger at me and said with a smile: "It was he that didn't want to continue!" I smiled back, embarrassed' (*EMH* 127).

[26] See Hsiao, *EMH* 126f; also *EMH* 125, *HAT* 97.

[27] Chang Chung-yuan, 'Tao: A New Way of Thinking', in *Journal of Chinese Philosophy* 1

is hardly susceptible of substantive proof, the fact remains that the question of influence cannot simply be dismissed. Indeed, an inquiry into this question recommends itself all the more.

Along with Hsiao, neither Parkes nor Pöggeler, nor even Cho, discounts some degree of influence, even though none of them has up to now adduced decisive evidence.[28] In his essay 'West-East Dialogue' Pöggeler simply surveys the extent of the relations between Heidegger's and East Asian thought, with primary reference to Petzet, Hsiao, and Fischer-Barnicol; after which he proceeds to discuss, sometimes in detail, the so-called parallels between East Asian thought (Daoism and Zen Buddhism) and Heidegger's later work. He concludes that Heidegger was in a position to incorporate impulses from the East Asian tradition into his own efforts at thinking, and thereby to provide a decisive stimulus for East-West dialogue. 'Heidegger', he says, 'has more than any other European philosopher initiated dialogue between the West and the Far East' (*HAT* 76). While Pöggeler appears to allow for a certain, rather vague, influence Parkes is more reticent with respect to this question: 'The question of influence – of Eastern thought on Heidegger's work – while interesting, is of secondary significance in comparison with the independent congruence of ideas' (*HAT* 2). He prefers to speak of a 'pre-established harmony' between Heidegger's thinking and Daoism and to emphasize 'the integrity of his thought' (*HAT* 9). In an important essay that is highly poetical and sparkles with detail, 'Thoughts on the Way: *Being and Time* via Lao-Chuang', Parkes successfully demonstrates the presence of a number of Daoist ideas (in particular) in *Being and Time*.[h] He proceeds from the assumption that *Being and Time* comes from a period antedating Heidegger's contact with Chinese philosophy (*HAT* 106, 109). And yet, when he returns elsewhere to the question of influence, he alleges in a rather careful formulation a certain influence from Chinese and Japanese philosophy on Heidegger's later work.[29] With regard to Heidegger's etymologizing and style tending towards the poetic, he concedes: 'In this he was surely influenced by his study of the Chinese language, and – given his years of contact with philosophers from Japan and his interest in Japanese culture generally – he probably also had some acquaintance with Dōgen's ideas' (p. 440).

(1974):137–52, 138; compare his slightly different, stronger formulation of a year later: 'Heidegger ... not only intellectually understands *Tao* but has intuitively experienced the essence of it as well' (*Tao: A New Way of Thinking*, ix). With respect to these remarks one must bear in mind that Chang had discussed the *Zhuangzi* with Heidegger in 1972 (see *PEW* 27:419) and was thus able to form his own impression as a competent interlocutor.
[28] See Cho, *Bewusstein und Natursein* 90. See also Wolfgang Schirmacher, 'Gelassenheit bei Schopenhauer und bei Heidegger', in *Schopenhauer Jahrbuch* 63 (1982):54–66, 61: 'The strong influence of "Eastern thought" on Schopenhauer as on Heidegger [!] is quite discernible in this definition of art'. The author is grateful for this reference to Mr Holger Krüger, MA, a doctoral candidate at the University of Düsseldorf.
[29] Graham Parkes, 'Dōgen/Heidegger/Dōgen: A Review of Dōgen Studies', *PEW* 37 (1987):437–54, 443. [See also the complementary essay below.]

2.3   As we see, the question of influence becomes more pressing as the indications accumulate. It is clearly a timely question from a number of perspectives, a question that can no longer be ignored, with many consequences for Heidegger-interpretation, the significance of which cannot as yet be fully evaluated. We must bear in mind, however, that (aside from Otto Pöggeler) Heidegger scholars have failed to take it seriously and have up to now taken care to exclude it, even though there have been sufficient grounds for raising it since Hsiao's report first appeared. It is possible that something Heidegger himself said has constituted a decisive obstacle to interest in the question first of all, and then to the development of a sense of its appropriateness. Heidegger made the following unequivocal statement in the well-known *Spiegel* interview:

> It is my conviction that a reversal can be prepared itself only from the same part of the world in which the modern technical world originated, and that it cannot come about through the adoption of Zen Buddhism or other Eastern experiences of the world. Rethinking requires the help of the European tradition and a reappropriation of it. Thinking is transformed only by thinking that has the same origin and destiny [*Bestimmung*].[30i]

The question of influence would now seem to be superfluous, having been thus settled *ex cathedra*, as it were. But it would appear to be much more appropriate to pay attention to so-called *meaning*ful (but simply fortuitous) parallels and to emphasize them in agreement with Heidegger. This would allow us to underscore, where applicable, the global significance of his thinking in a fitting manner. Why, then, should Heidegger have simply dismissed 'Eastern experiences of the world' if he himself incorporated some of them constructively in his work and in a most significant way?[j] Serious consideration of the question of influence then meets with incomprehension and has to reckon with considerable difficulties. Aside from this dismissal on Heidegger's part, there is in the texts published so far no *direct* reference to the fact that he gained significant stimulus and constant inspiration from East Asian thought – or that he found anything of worth there at all. Outside his works, he did at least say to Fischer-Barnicol that while he had worked with Japanese from early on, he had learned more from the Chinese (*EMH* 102).

3   Given what we have seen so far, the following four points speak in favour of dealing with the question of influence: first, Heidegger's demonstrated fondness for the Daoist ideas in the *Laozi* and *Zhuangzi*, especially

---

[30] 'Only a God Can Save Us' (*Der Spiegel*'s interview with Martin Heidegger, 1966, published 1976), translated by Maria P. Alter and John D. Caputo, in Richard Wolin, ed., *The Heidegger Controversy: A Critical Reader* (Cambridge, Mass. and London 1993), 91–116, 113. [As usual, my translation is directly from the German original (see endnote 'i').]

in the Buber edition, and his many competent conversation-partners on East Asian topics; second, the collaboration with Hsiao, requested and followed through by Heidegger, on translating the *Laozi* into German, and the valuable acquaintance with East Asian thought that he gleaned from the project; third, the large number of parallels that have since been discerned, especially with the later work; fourth, Heidegger's characteristic paraphrasing or poetic rewriting of an excerpt from Chapter 15 of the *Laozi*.

Under the circumstances, one cannot dismiss the possibility that Heidegger intentionally incorporated East Asian ideas, in an encoded manner, into his work. The question of influence is therefore by no means superfluous, and it is engaged in the study that follows. The investigation does not presume to lead to results that are final and definite; indeed, it is not in a position to offer a treatment that is even half-way exhaustive. Something like that could possibly be effected only by an intercultural team-project that would undertake an exegesis of every text in the entire Heidegger corpus (which is still not available). But the present study aims to provide a stimulus and sufficient new impulses to prompt further investigations of this kind. It would thereby also strengthen the kind of comparative philosophical research into foundations that is necessary these days, and which would naturally take into account non-Western philosophical thinking.

2 The 'Conversation'

1 Heidegger's text 'From a Conversation on Language' with the subtitle 'Between a Japanese and an Inquirer', which appears as the third of six texts in *Unterwegs zur Sprache*,[k] constitutes a remarkable exception in the work that has been published so far. For he not only deals here, in the form of a dialogue, with the nature of language (from a Western perspective), but also discusses related themes to do with East Asian culture.[31] It is by no means one of Heidegger's more comprehensible texts; quite the opposite. Its difficulty is attested to by the apparent absence of any comprehensive interpretation of it, or even an adequate appreciation. Graham Parkes is a welcome exception here, though only in so far as he briefly explicates an important transcultural issue raised by the Japanese word for language, *kotoba* (*HAT* 213–16). Otherwise, there are only occasional references in Western languages to this 'Conversation', which one can rank without hesitation among the richest and most significant texts of Heidegger's to have appeared up to now.

This text has, of course, been translated into Japanese, by the renowned Japanese Germanist Tezuka Tomio. Tezuka not only appended a long explanatory afterword to his translation, but also provided a detailed account (in Japanese) of his conversation with the author under the title 'An Hour with Heidegger'. This account is extremely valuable in helping us to understand and interpret the content of the 'Conversation', and moreover it also provides a number of reference points that illuminate possible contexts for the genesis of the text. Since it is probably unknown to the majority of Heidegger scholars in the West, a translation of Tezuka's report has been provided in Chapter 7.[32]

---

[31] According to Petzet, this text is among those that were important to Heidegger himself (P 166/175).
[32] A dual-language version of the translation has been available since October 1988: Tomio Tezuka, 'An Hour with Heidegger', Japanese/German, translated from the Japanese and with an afterword by Reinhard May.

2.1 According to Tezuka's report, Heidegger's interest in Japan was stimulated by his association with the Japanese philosopher Kuki Shūzō,[33] he had Tezuka explicate a haiku by Bashō for him, and he was also interested in Zen thought.[1] We learn further that Heidegger inquired about the Japanese word for language. He immediately committed to paper Tezuka's explanation, which appeared to fit with his own ideas, and noted that the meaning of the Japanese word for language was *thing*. Tezuka's response to this interpretation was, however, somewhat reticent. The conversation then came around, in accordance with Heidegger's wishes, to the special nature of Japanese art.

In the further course of the conversation, the first half of which was taken up more or less by Tezuka's answering Heidegger's questions, the latter wanted to know what expressions there were in everyday Japanese for 'appearance' and 'essence' (or for 'thing' and 'thingness'). He greeted Tezuka's profound and philosophically rich responses with constant interest and again committed them to paper. Before eventually inviting Tezuka to pose some questions, Heidegger made a revealing remark that emphasized his delight with the former's explanations: 'East and West must engage in dialogue at this deep level. It is useless to do interviews that merely deal with one superficial phenomenon after another'.[34] Soon thereafter the first half of the conversation between Heidegger and Tezuka was over.

2.2 Tezuka's report was first published in Japan in 1955 and is a valuable document for our purposes, in so far as it figures in a series of consequential conversations Heidegger had with East Asian scholars. It also shows how highly Heidegger valued East Asian culture and how deeply it interested him.

The report gives the impression of a conversation conducted on a sophisticated level, and yet a conversation that is by no means identical with the one Heidegger presented in 1959 in *On the Way to Language*. He probably regarded the highly concentrated conversation as an opportunity to put some well-pondered questions to his Japanese guest, whose command of German was extraordinarily good. He took down Tezuka's answers on the spot in writing, possibly for the purposes of a subsequent elaboration of a text of his own. The Chinese philosopher Paul Hsiao described a similar procedure when he looked back on his collaboration

---

[33] Heidegger often mentions Count Kuki (1888–1941). For more about Kuki, see Hakoishi Masayuki, 'Die Phänomenologie in Japan', *Zeitschrift für Philosophische Forschung* 37 (1983):299–315, 304.

[34] Quoted in Japanese by Tezuka ('An Hour with Heidegger', p. 164); see p. 62 below. Compare Heidegger, 'A Dialogue on Language', in *WL* 8; 'Aus einem Gespräch von der Sprache', in *US* 94. [Subsequent references to this latter text in the present chapter will be made simply by means of the page numbers of the English translation and the German original respectively.]

with him: 'Heidegger essentially asked questions and continued to ask unremittingly, penetratingly, relentlessly, about every possible meaning-context that could be conceived of in the mysterious interplay of symbolic relations' (*EMH* 126).

When one examines what Tezuka writes in the explanatory after-word to his translation of the 'Conversation'[35] and carefully compares Heidegger's text with the former's report of their conversation, it becomes immediately clear that Heidegger has *invented* a challenging dialogue by utilizing a variety of relevant pieces of information and appropriate textual excerpts. For with the exception of a very few passages in Heidegger's text, there is nothing approaching even an approximate reproduction of the conversation he actually had with Tezuka. There is thus hardly any 'authenticity' to the 'Conversation' whatsoever. For example, Heidegger inquired about the literary origins of Kurosawa's film *Rashōmon*: in the 'Conversation', by contrast, it is the 'Japanese' who adduces this film as 'a perfect example' of what the 'Inquirer' disparagingly calls the 'Europeanization of human being and the earth, which is sapping every-thing essential at its source' (16/104). The subsequent remarks about *Rashōmon* also have very little to do with the actual conversation. The same is true for most of the rest of Heidegger's text, which must draw on other materials.

2.3 The conversation with Tezuka appears to have been a welcome source of inspiration for Heidegger in a number of respects, while it also provided several starting-points for typically Heideggerian formula-tions. The result, *his* 'conversation', is thus an unusual presentation of Heidegger's ideas.

Under these circumstances it is not improbable that the shrewdly chosen title of the 'Conversation' could tempt us to regard this 'conversation' as a quasi-authentic dialogue between a 'Japanese' acting *in propria persona* and an 'Inquirer' – Heidegger himself – and to treat it accordingly. In the secondary literature up to now, almost everybody has proceeded on the assumption that in 'From a Conversation on Language – between a Japanese and an Inquirer' the part of the 'Japanese' stems from that very person, or that it at least refers to him in the essentials.[36] In any case, it has apparently not been suggested that the text represents exclusively Heidegger's own work, and that all passages in it are thus to be ascribed to Heidegger himself.

---

[35] Tezuka Tomio, 'Kaisetsu' (Commentary), in *Haidegga zenshū* 21:137–50.
[36] Pöggeler also (*HAT* 50, 70, 72) seems to have proceeded from this assumption. Parkes is a little more circumspect in his evaluation, even if he assumes that 'both dialogues [the other being the 'Feldweggespräch' in *Gelassenheit* (the 'Conversation on a Country Path' in *Discourse on Thinking*)] were based on actual conversations, but were considerably reworked by Heidegger' (*HAT* 139f). Elisabeth Feist Hirsch holds a similar view (*PEW* 20:247). See also the review of *Unterwegs zur Sprache* by Walter Uhsadel in *Theologische Literaturzeitung* 3 (1961):217–21, 220.

Aside from the illumination provided by Tezuka, there is presumably only one indication in the secondary literature in the West that goes to the heart of the (hardly transparent) matter without misunderstanding. The Japanese author Michiko Yoneda discusses it in her book *Gespräch und Dichtung* (*Conversation and Poetry*), in so far as she maintains, with direct reference to Tezuka's explanatory afterword to his translation, that the 'Conversation' is Heidegger's own work.[37] We are thus talking about an astonishing work that could well be furnished with this motto from Heidegger: 'East and West must engage in dialogue at this kind of depth'. This sentence of Heidegger's, which was subsequently transposed into an invented dialogue, was recounted word for word by Tezuka.[38] It is understandable that this text has posed many problems for readers and interpreters of Heidegger on account of the strangeness of many passages in it, which is no doubt why it has been largely ignored.

2.4 As for the history of the genesis of 'From a Conversation on Language – Between a Japanese and an Inquirer', Heidegger gives (as he often does) an indication, at the end of the volume *On the Way to Language*. The note reads: 'The text, which has remained unpublished for some time, originated in 1953/54, and was occasioned by a visit from Professor Tezuka of the Imperial University of Tokyo' (199/269). The note is clearly incomplete and inaccurate – but it can obviously be transformed by a harmless operation on its sentence structure, in which the *title* of the text is simply inserted at a particular point in the text of the *note*. Such a (re)construction provides the full information, which was communicated indirectly (in code), in the following clearly formulated sentence:

> The text, which has remained unpublished for some time, originated *from a conversation on language between a Japanese and an Inquirer* in 1953/54, and was occasioned by a visit from Professor Tezuka of the Imperial University of Tokyo.ᵐ

As we now know from Tezuka, however, his visit did not take place until March 1954, so we might well ask what prompted Heidegger to make the date so vague when, in fact, he knew it more precisely. Whatever his motivation might have been, it is unimportant for our present purposes. What is certain is that Heidegger composed a remarkable dialogue and published it under a title that could easily lead to the assessments that have generally been made of it.

[37] Michiko Yoneda, *Gespräch und Dichtung: Ein Auseinandersetzungsversuch der Sprachauffassung Heideggers mit einem japanischen Sagen* (Frankfurt aM/Bern/New York 1984), 91. I am grateful to Professor Kawahara (Tokyo) for bringing this work to my attention.
[38] Aside from Plato, whose dialogues Heidegger, significantly, mentions in the 'Conversation' (52/151), the masterful dialogues of David Hume and Arthur Schopenhauer come to mind, both of whom had good reasons for 'packaging' their ideas about religion in this form.

3 Let us now turn briefly to the content of the 'Conversation'. Heidegger treats two main topics in this pseudo-dialogue: first, the idea of *iki*, in connection with questions about the aesthetics and special nature of East Asian (Japanese) art; and second, the nature of language, in connection with the Japanese word for language, *kotoba*. By the way, as it were, large parts of the text present the reader with a striking mixture of biographical self-portrayal and wide-ranging self-interpretation, often looking back far into the past, in which discussions of East Asian thinking play a not insignificant role. Points of contact between the account of Tezuka and Heidegger's composition are to be found at only a few places in the text: once in the characterization of East Asian (Japanese) art and poetry in terms of *iro* and *kū*, as well as *kū* and *mu*, and again with respect to *kotoba* (language), where Heidegger orchestrates the characterization of what is 'said' by *kotoba* as the high point of the conversation. In both cases, rather than adopting Tezuka's explanations directly, he paraphrased them into his text in his own way. There is a similar situation with the reference to the film *Rashōmon*. In contrast with the actual conversation, Heidegger now has the 'Japanese' make this reference. The theme of East-West dialogue is likewise 'dialogized' and positioned skilfully in the text, as is illustrated by the following detailed example that is revelatory for our investigation.

> *Inquirer:* The prospects for a thinking that strives to correspond to the nature of language still remains concealed in their vast entirety.[n] Thus I don't yet see whether what I am trying to think as the nature [*Wesen*] of language is *also* adequate to the nature of East Asian language (8/93–4). – Especially since the *nature* of language [*Sprach*wesen] remains something completely different [*ein durchaus anderes*] for East Asian and European peoples (23/113). – In any case my concern was to make visible, however obscurely – if not confusedly – sensed, that which is quite different [*das ganz Andere*] (34–5/128). – Whether in the end, which would also be the beginning, a nature of language can reach the thinking experience which would enable European-occidental and East Asian saying to come into conversation in such a way that something sings which wells up from a single source (8/94). – *Japanese:* ... such that at times a light shone for me that made me suspect that the essential source of the two fundamentally different languages was the same (24/115). – *I:* ... wells up from a single source. – *J:* That would then, however, remain hidden from both language worlds. – *I:* That is what I mean (8/94).

It is easy to see that the 'Conversation' can be read in large part as a monologue.

Count Kuki plays a disproportionately major role in Heidegger's text unlike in the actual conversation, at least according to Tezuka's report. Tezuka's conversation with Heidegger did not originate from reminiscences of Kuki, and it was not Tezuka but rather Heidegger who brought the conversation around to that topic. Heidegger apparently spoke warmly of Kuki, and this also comes across in the 'Conversation'.[39] There Heidegger has the 'Japanese' bring up the topic of Kuki at the beginning of the conversation. In the course of the text the talk repeatedly comes round to Kuki in the appropriate context; but none of this has anything to do with Tezuka, who was not, in fact, personally acquainted with Kuki but was only, by his own testimony, a reader of his works.[40o] As for *iki*, a major theme of Heidegger's text, Tezuka and Heidegger did not speak of it at all, and so Heidegger's acquaintance with the idea must come from other sources. Whether he reproduced the relevant topics faithfully is a different question, to which we shall return when we deal with his interpretation of *iki*.

In so far as the text alludes to what actually occurred, especially with respect to the not unimportant role of Count Kuki, there is still a great deal to clarify and, where necessary, correct. For our purposes, it is sufficient for the time being to suppose in general that we are dealing with a mixture of *invention* and *truth*, in which it is by no means easy to separate one from the other.[p] But this may lie in the very nature of Heidegger's pseudo-dialogue, which presents a further remarkable piece of self-interpretation.

4   Let us now look at two instances of the way in which Heidegger paraphrases (and embellishes) his own knowledge and Tezuka's explanations of the special nature of Japanese thinking and integrates them into his dialogue.

First, Tezuka emphasizes 'that the kind of *indefiniteness* conveyed by this film [*Rashōmon*] concerning our knowledge of reality may have intrigued Heidegger as an East Asian phenomenon' (62 below). The appropriateness of Tezuka's surmise is confirmed by Heidegger's own formulation, in that he has *his* 'Japanese' speak of '[The danger] that we [Japanese] may be misled by the conceptual richness offered by the spirit of European language into disparaging that which lays claim to our existence [*Dasein*] as something indefinite and ephemeral' (3/88). A later passage reads: 'We Japanese are not disconcerted when a conversation leaves indefinite [*im Unbestimmten*] what is really meant, or even shelters it back in the indefinable [*ins Unbestimmbare*]' (13/100).

Second, Tezuka explained to Heidegger, at the latter's request, the meanings of the Japanese words *shiki* and *kū*: 'To characterize the meanings of these words in more detail, *shiki* would be colour and colouring [*iro*], and, by extension, appearance; and though *kū* originally means

---

[39] 'Conversation' 4/89. This stands in contrast, however, to another of Heidegger's remarks about Kuki, as reported by Fischer-Barnicol: 'By the way Count Kuki must have learned German only when he got to Paris' (*EMH* 102) – a remark that does not do justice to Kuki's known language abilities.

[40] Tezuka,'Kaisetsu', 141.

emptiness, or sky (*sora*), it also means *the Open* (*the opened-up world*)' (below).

Heidegger was especially pleased by this explanation. In his text Tezuka's presentation is given in the following variations: 'We say *iro*, colour, and *kū*, emptiness, the Open, sky. We say: Without *iro* no *kū*' (14/102).[q] And then several lines later: '*Iro* does name colour, and yet it means essentially more than whatever is perceivable by the senses. *Kū* does name emptiness and the Open, and yet it means something other than just the suprasensible' (15/102). Later in the course of the text Heidegger has the 'Japanese' go on to say: 'Farness [*Weite*] is the limitless [*Grenzenlose*] that is shown us in *kū*, which means the emptiness of the sky' (41/137). With this last formulation, which apparently wants to emphasize *the limitless* for some reason (as we shall see in Chapters 3 and 5), Heidegger strains the limits of paraphrase and also blurs the appropriately drawn contours of the *shiki soku ze kū* way of thinking (the *rūpa-śūnyatā* way of thinking in Mahāyāna Buddhism).[41] Earlier there is another passage in the interchange between *I* and *J* that has nothing to do with the actual conversation between Heidegger and Tezuka but does something to advance the pseudo-dialogue: – '*I*: Your suggestions, which I can follow only from a distance, increase my unease. . . . – *J*: You mean [the conversation] could bring us closer to what is unsaid? – *I*: Abundant food for thought would thereby be granted to us' (15/102–3).

In both cases we encounter the kind of paraphrasing technique familiar to us from the case of Hsiao's translation of Chapter 15 of the *Laozi* and Heidegger's own subsequent version of it. What is new here is the nature and scope of the textual appropriation, which we shall see again elsewhere. Here Heidegger weaves two passages from a foreign text almost verbatim into his 'Conversation', ignoring the practice of indicating the source precisely. Inconspicuously and by the way, and yet inserted into a context already prepared, Heidegger mentions Oscar Benl's Academy Treatise on Noh drama and invents (presumably) the following statement, which he puts in the mouth of the 'Japanese': 'In [our] opinion that is a most thorough piece of work and quite the best thing you could read on the Noh drama' (17–18/106). There then follows a skilful transition to the complex problematic of emptiness, nothingness, and Heidegger's attempt to overcome metaphysics – to a lengthy (and encoded) passage that is apparently meant to contribute, as an important piece of self-interpretation, to the understanding of his texts. The (dramaturgical) reference to Benl seems thereby to have served its purpose, at least until over forty pages later, when two passages from Benl's text turn up in Heidegger's 'Conversation' with no further indication of the source.

[41] See, for example, the *Prajñā-pāramitā-hṛdaya-sūtra*, in *Buddhist Mahāyāna Texts*, part 2, in F. Max Müller, ed., *The Sacred Books of the East* 49:147–9, 153–4.

The evidence points to Benl's 'Zeami Motokiyo and the Spirit of Noh Drama: Esoteric Aesthetic Writings from the Fifteenth Century' from 1952.[42] Heidegger uses this text for his pseudo-dialogue in three ways.

First, Benl discusses Zeami (an actor, playwright, and critic: 1363–1443), who writes in his work of the nature and effect of 'the mystery' [*Geheimnis*]. A passage there reads as follows:

> It is not sufficient not to reveal [the mystery], one must not let the others even suspect that one possesses a mystery (Benl, 192).

Heidegger's version reads:

> A mystery is only a mystery as long as it does not come to light *that* there is a mystery (50/148).[r]

He has the 'Japanese' speak these lines.

Second, later in his text Benl quotes verbatim an ancient Japanese poem, and in a footnote he gives the name of the author in romanization as well as Chinese characters. In parallel with the original version of the poem in romanization Benl gives a literal translation:

> To smell a plum blossom / In a cherry blossom / And let both bloom / On a willow branch – thus would I wish it (Benl, 202).

Heidegger makes his own version of this by having his 'Japanese' say:

> In our ancient Japanese poetry an unknown poet sings of the inter- mingling fragrance of the cherry and plum blossom on the same branch (53/153).[s]

What is striking about Heidegger's version is that he actually has the 'Japanese' speak of an 'unknown' poet, even though he knew the poet's name perfectly well from Benl's footnote – namely, Nakahara Tokinori.[43]

The correspondences are unambiguous and, given their content, can hardly have occurred fortuitously. There can be no doubt that in both cases we are dealing with passages that Heidegger has modified slightly and skilfully integrated into his pseudo-dialogue.

Third, for his interpretation of *iki* Heidegger apparently looked to Benl for assistance, but in an inappropriate text. For Heidegger's interpreta- tion of *iki* can hardly be squared with Kuki's understanding of the idea. Heidegger, with the poet working more than the thinker, has his 'Japanese' say: '*Iki* is the gracious [*das Anmutende*]' (43/140). He then makes a tran-

---

[42] Oscar Benl, 'Seami Motokiyo und der Geist des Nō-Schauspiels: Geheime kunstkritische Schriften aus dem 15. Jahrhundert', in *Akademie der Wissenschaften und der Literatur, Abhandlungen der Klasse der Literatur* 1952, no. 5 (Wiesbaden 1953):103–249.

[43] In note 16 of his Japanese translation of the 'Conversation' (p. 136) Tezuka, who did not mention this poem in his conversation with Heidegger, cites on the basis of surmise (not knowing Benl's treatise) Nakahara Tokinori and his poem, which he reproduces in the orig- inal for the benefit of the Japanese reader.

sition by adducing, among other things, Schiller's *Anmut und Würde* ('Grace and Dignity'), in order to 'remove *iki* – now translated as "grace" – from the realm of aesthetics and the subject–object relationship' (44/141), and to present it in the following quasi-poetical formulation: '– *J*: *Iki* is the breath of the stillness of luminous rapture'. Which the *I* elaborates by saying: 'You are then taking the rapture literally as a drawing away, an attraction – into stillness'.

This has nothing whatever to do with *iki*, which means, rather, 'chic' or 'elegance', or, as an adjective, 'elegant, chic, delicate, smart, pretty, refined, tasteful'.[44] Michiko Yoneda supposes that Heidegger is here interpolating *iki* in the sense of (Bashō's notion of) *fūga*.[1] But there are good grounds for supposing that Heidegger is instead drawing on Benl's text in connection with Schiller's *Anmut und Würde*, where Benl refers to 'grace' in the context of explaining the Japanese term *yūgen*.[45] Heidegger's 'breath of the stillness of luminous rapture' probably has its inspiration from a combination of formulations by Benl.[46]

We encounter a substantive inaccuracy – one could even say distortion – in Heidegger's interpretation of the Japanese word for 'language', *kotoba*, where he renders the character for *ba* (*ha*) in *kotoba* as 'blossom petals' in order to establish a semantic relationship with the 'cherry and plum blossoms on the same branch', and thereby to achieve at the end of the 'Conversation' an especially fine effect with the passage already mentioned, and at the same time to prepare a comparison with one of his own characteristic formulations.[47] In this case, too, the work of the poet rather than the philosopher comes to the fore, albeit under the influence of the Benl treatise.[48] For Tezuka speaks only of the word's meaning leaves of trees and not blossom petals (60 below), though the latter suit Heidegger better as far as composition is concerned.

---

[44] H. Okutsu, *Neues Japanisch-Deutsches Wörterbuch* (Tokyo 1959, 1982), 461. See Hakoishi, who comments on a long passage from Kuki's book *The Structure of 'Iki'* (1930, [14] 1969) by saying, 'He [Kuki] arrives at the conclusion: '"Coquetry" that is reconciled to its fate, in other words, the way of living that is free with the spirit that will not bend: that is Iki' ('Die Phänomenologie in Japan', 304f). Compare Yoneda, *Gespräch und Dichtung*, 93f [who remarks on the utter inappropriateness of the translations of *iki* offered in Heidegger's text]. The question of how far Heidegger's etymological explanation of the word 'rapture' [*Entzücken*] is at all tenable can be left aside for now.
[45] See Benl, 'Seami Motokiyo' 180, 221, 244 (108, 178f, 180, 220).
[46] Ibid. 108, 175, 232, 244.
[47] See *WL* 45/*US* 142, and also 47/144, 48/146, 53/153.
[48] See Benl, 'Seami Motokiyo' 127ff, 232f. Compare also Wilhelm von Humboldt, 'Uber die Verschiedenheit des menschlichen Sprachbaues und ihren Einfluss auf die geistige Entwicklung des Menschengeschlechts [1830–1835]', in *Wilhelm von Humboldt, Schriften zur Sprachphilosophie*, Flitner and Giel, eds (Darmstadt 1963), 3:368–756, 449: 'The simple word is the consummate blossom that buds from [language]' (*Akademie-Ausgabe* 1903–36, 7:73) [*On Language: The Diversity of Human Language-Structure and its Influence on the Mental Development of Mankind*, translated by Peter Heath (Cambridge 1988), 70]. This reference also should not be overlooked in connection with the role played by this work [of Humboldt's] in Heidegger's *On the Way to Language* in general.

5   We shall return to Heidegger's 'Conversation' later (in Chapter 5); but before we do, let us look at one more instance of Heidegger's freely poetic way of dealing with East Asian thought. In this case, it is not improbable that Heidegger is taking up a key idea from the *Laozi* and incorporating it into his text at an appropriate point – a *topos* that he had already worked with in a significant way[u] in the 'Letter on Humanism'. In chapter 41 of the *Laozi* we read: '*Dao* [way] is hidden and nameless'.[49] In what appears to be an allusion to this idea, Heidegger gives in his 'Conversation' this very telling and instructive formulation: 'This was not done, as many people think, in order to deny the importance of phenomenology, but in order to leave my way of thinking in the nameless' (29/121, cf. 138). In the 'Letter on Humanism' (1946, first published in 1947) he writes, just as tellingly: 'But if the human being is to find its way once again into the nearness of Being, it must first learn to exist in the nameless'.[50]

[49] [*Tao ist verborgen, namenlos.*] In the translation by Victor von Strauss (*Lao-Tse, Tao Tê King: Aus dem Chinesischen übersetzt und kommentiert von Victor von Strauss* [Leipzig 1870; Zürich 1959]), 113; compare also Chapters 1, 14, 21, 25, 32, 37.

[50] 'Letter on Humanism', in *Basic Writings*, edited by David Farrell Krell (New York 1977), 193–242, 199; 'Brief über den "Humanismus"', in *WM* (Frankfurt a.M. 1967), 145–94, 150. Compare 'The Thinker as Poet': 'The saying [*Sage* – way/*dao*; see Chapter 4] of thinking would be stilled in its being only by becoming incapable of saying that which must remain unspoken' (*Poetry, Language and Thought* [henceforth '*PLT*'], translated by Albert Hofstadter (New York 1971), 1–14, 11; 'Aus der Erfahrung des Denkens', in *GA* 13:75–86, 83. Compare also 'Conversation on a Country Path about Thinking', in *Discourse on Thinking* (henceforth '*DT*'), translated by John M. Anderson and E. Hans Freund (New York 1966), 58–90, 70f; 'Zur Erörterung der Gelassenheit', in *GA* 13:37–74, 52f (Neske edition, 45f).

3 Nothing, emptiness, and the clearing

1.1 In order to pursue the supposition of further correspondences between Heidegger's thinking and Daoist ideas, we turn to three central topics [*Topoi*] that are found again and again in his work.[51] Our first concern is with the *topos* 'Nothing' [*das Nichts*], which runs significantly [*wegweisend*] through Heidegger's work like a red thread, and ultimately distinguishes itself from everything else that has been thought and said in Western philosophy about the topic of Nothing.

We shall trace Heidegger's lines of thinking primarily through formulations that he himself chose with careful consideration. We shall thereby find that to clarify the path of his thinking (Denk*weg*) he elucidates certain major ideas repeatedly, and in an especially striking way in his later texts, thus interpreting his own work.[52] One should therefore pay close attention to these characteristic elucidations of his major ideas.

We encounter Heidegger's major guiding [*wegweisend*] idea already in the context of 'the elaboration [and answering] of the question of the meaning of "*Being*", in the following formulation: 'The Being of beings "is" not itself a being'.[53] What is it then, for Heidegger? It is *nothing*. Heidegger eventually says, 'Nothing is the characteristic [*Kennzeichnung*] of Being'.[54] Or, even more clearly: 'Being: Nothing: Same'.[55v]

---

[51] There are good grounds for talking of *topoi* in this context, in so far as Heidegger's major ideas are appropriately understood as places along a way, as *topoi* on the path of his thinking. See Otto Pöggeler, 'Sein als Ereignis', *Zeitschrift für Philosophische Forschung* 13 (1959):597–632, who understands Heidegger's later thinking especially in the sense of a 'topology' (630). See also Pöggeler's *Martin Heidegger's Path of Thinking* (Atlantic Highlands 1987), esp. 257, note 57.

[52] See Friedrich Wilhelm von Herrmann, *Die Selbstinterpretation Martin Heideggers* (Meisenheim am Glan 1964), 5–9.

[53] *Sein und Zeit* [henceforth '*SZ*'], 1, 6. Subsequent references to this text will be to the standard text published by Niemeyer, since the pagination of this edition is given in the margins of both the English translation by Macquarrie and Robinson, *Being and Time*, and the *Gesamtausgabe* edition (*GA* 2).

[54] 'Seminar in Le Thor, 1969' [henceforth 'SLT'], in *Vier Seminare* (Frankfurt a.M. 1977), 64–109, 101.

[55] 'SLT' 101, 99. See also 'Was ist Metaphysik?' (in *GA* 9), 115, note c, 106, note b; 'The Age of the World Picture', in *QT* 154; *Martin Heidegger im Gespräch*, ed. Richard Wisser (Freiburg/Munich 1970), 75.

Heidegger reaches this result over the course of many stages of formulation. On the way, and in reversing the question of Being, as it were, he also deals with (and answers) the question of Nothing. The inquiry into the 'meaning of Being', which for him has been forgotten and so 'still remains' to be answered (*SZ* 21, 230), is at the same time an inquiry into Nothing, and into the meaning of Nothing in contrast to the nothingness of nihilism. Thus in both aspects of the inquiry the task of the 'true over-coming of nihilism' comes to the fore.[56] Heidegger employs the following formulations, which, when read serially, give unequivocal expression to his conclusions:

> Nothingness ... reveals itself as belonging [*zugehörig*] to the Being of beings. ... This Nothing [of beings] 'works' [*west*] as Being. ... That which is not a being [is] Nothing understood as Being itself.[57]

Supplementing the formulations in *Being and Time* (21, 35), Heidegger remarks moreover: 'The essential origin [*Wesensherkunft*] of the Being of beings has not been properly thought'.[58] By contrast with Being, which for Heidegger is 'not any kind of being' (*SZ* 4), one understands by *beings* everything 'that we can in any way mean'.[59] As for Being, he explains: 'Being "is" no more than Nothing "is". But *it gives* [Es gibt] both' (*QB* 97).[w] And he later suggests, with reference to the simple expression 'Being: Nothing', that 'it is better to give up the "is" here' ('SLT' 85). As early as 1935 Heidegger expresses a similar thought, though not as clearly as in later formulations: 'But Being remains untraceable, almost like Nothing, or in the end *exactly* [ganz] like it. ... The Other to it [Being] is only Nothing' (*IM* 35/27, 79/60).

In the course of striving to clarify his understanding of Being and Nothing in the 1969 Le Thor seminar, Heidegger supplements the older formulations from 1946 on with new ones that are basically indistinguishable as far as content is concerned. Some of these we have already seen and can tell from them how superbly Heidegger employs his subtle, productive, and elegant paraphrasing technique. Let us clarify this point by considering a few more examples, which will also help us to understand his thinking better.

In a direct inquiry into Being, Heidegger writes in the 'Letter on Humanism': 'And yet Being – what is Being? It is It itself' (*BW* 210/*Wm*

[56] *An Introduction to Metaphysics* [henceforth '*IM*'], translated by Ralph Mannheim (New Haven/London 1959), 203; *Einführung in die Metaphysik*, 155.

[57] 'What Is Metaphysics?', in *BW* 110/*Wm* 16–17; compare *IM* 85/64; 'Nachwort zu: "Was ist Metaphysik?"', in *Wm* 99–108, 101–2; 'Introduction to "What Is Metaphysics?"', in Walter Kaufmann, *Existentialism from Dostoevsky to Sartre* (New York 1957), 207–21, 221/ 'Einleitung zu: "Was ist Metaphysik?"', in *Wm* 195–211, 211.

[58] 'Was heisst Denken?', in *Vorträge und Aufsätze* [henceforth '*VA*'] (Pfullingen 1954), 2:3–17, 17.

[59] Friedrich Wilhelm von Herrmann, *Hermeneutische Phänomenologie des Daseins: Eine Erläuterung von 'Sein und Zeit'*, vol. 1 (Frankfurt aM 1987), 68.

162). With respect to Nothing this can be formulated as: 'Being as ~~Being~~' (*QB* 33; cf. 81f, 89–91).ˣ A later explanatory remark, intended to obviate any misunderstanding, reads as follows: '[The idea] that Being is not absolutely for itself [*für sich*] is diametrically opposed to Hegel' ('SLT' 108). With this Heidegger distinguishes himself from Hegel unequivocally.[60] As for the further difference between Heidegger and the Presocratics (Parmenides in particular), this would ultimately be as important as that between Heidegger and Hegel.[61]

Heidegger's position with respect to the context articulated here is quite unique in the Western tradition. This point is further emphasized by the expressions he uses to describe Nothing in order to assimilate it to other *topoi*, and yet without affecting or undermining the *new* sense of Being and Nothing. He justifies his procedure by way of a detailed and very telling reference to Wilhelm von Humboldt. On being asked, in the Le Thor seminar, whether his use of old expressions for a new thinking is able to characterize this new thinking adequately – 'How far is it possible to use the same terms both within and outside metaphysics?' – Heidegger refers to the last page of *On the Way to Language* and repeats the citation [of Humboldt] he made there: 'Another meaning is then installed in the same housing [*Gehäuse*], something different is conveyed in the same coinage, and a differently graduated train of ideas is indicated according to the same laws of connection'.[62]

In the following passages Heidegger puts 'presencing' [*Anwesen*] in place of 'Being' [*Sein*] and 'unconcealedness' [*Unverborgenheit*] in place of 'Nothing' [*Nichts*] (and vice versa), thereby elucidating the new 'sense' of the old 'housing':

> The enigma is ... 'Being'. For that reason 'Being' remains simply the provisional word. Let us see to it that our thinking does not simply follow it blindly. Let us first ponder the fact that 'Being' is originally called 'presencing', and 'presencing' means: to come to and endure in unconcealedness'.[63]y

---

[60] Heidegger had already emphasized the *belonging together* of Nothing and Being, which do not, in contrast to the Hegelian conception of thinking, 'come together [thanks to their] indefiniteness and immediacy' ('What is Metaphysics?', in *BW* 110/*Wm* 17). See also *IM* 85/64.

[61] Ernst Tugendhat has distinguished Hegel's language from Heidegger's in this respect and has articulated the significant differences – with respect to Parmenides as well ('Das Sein und das Nichts', in *Durchblicke – Martin Heidegger zum 80. Geburtstag* [Frankfurt a.M. 1970], 132–61, 156–60, 134–46.) There can be no doubt that Heidegger also wanted to distinguish himself from the German mystics of the Middle Ages and succeeded in so doing, even though there are distinct resonances with them here and there.

[62] 'SLT' 87–8; referring to the end of 'The Way to Language', in *WL* 136/*US* 268. Von Humboldt, *On Language* 87/'Ueber die Verschiedenheit des menschlichen Sprachbaues', 472 (*Akademie-Ausgabe* 7:93); translation modified. [See also footnote 125 below.]

[63] 'Logos', in *Early Greek Thinking*, translated by David Farrell Krell and Frank A. Capuzzi (New York 1975), 59–78, 78. Compare 'What Are Poets For?', in *PLT* 93; 'Was heisst

Presencing occurs [*ereignet sich*] only where unconcealedness already holds sway.[64]

Nothing belongs . . . as absence [*ab-wesend*] to presencing [Being] (*QB* 87/*Wm* 241).

Presencing [*An-wesen*] needs and uses [*braucht*] the Open of a clearing [*Lichtung*] (*ID* 31/19).

To let-presence means: to reveal [*Entbergen*], to bring into the Open. In revealing there plays a giving, one that in *letting*-presence [*Anwesen-lassen*] gives presencing, or Being (*TB* 5/5).

In each case Heidegger substitutes one for the other, 'Nothing' for 'Being' (and, for 'Being', 'presence') and vice versa, and thereby effects permanent translations: for 'Nothing' now also 'unconcealedness', the 'Open', and the 'clearing'. Another term that belongs to this sequence of correspondences is 'truth' in the sense of 'Being', 'Nothing', and 'uncon-cealedness'. In *Being and Time* Heidegger writes, 'Being and truth "are" equiprimordial' (*SZ* 230); while he later also takes 'Nothing' and 'Being' to be equiprimordial in the formulation: 'to think *that* Nothing that is equiprimordially the Same as Being'.[65]

These kinds of obvious correspondences, which are easily to be found throughout Heidegger's work and represent essential factors in its design, always concern his major thought, namely 'Nothing', which constitutes unmistakably (as we have seen already in the case of *Being and Time*) the 'meaning of Being'. Thus Heidegger makes a clear distinction between this idea and what he calls 'empty nothing'[66] or also nugatory nothing [*das nichtige Nichts*]. By contrast: 'This [true] Nothing . . . is nothing nugatory [*nichts Nichtiges*]. It belongs to presencing [Being]. Being and Nothing are not given beside one another. Each uses itself on behalf of the other in a relationship whose essential richness we have hardly begun to ponder' (*QB* 97/*Wm* 247).

These interpretations of 'Nothing' have, for Heidegger, nothing to do with nihilism as it has been understood so far (since Nietzsche); their aim is rather the overcoming of nihilism. There can be no misunderstanding here, since Heidegger states as early as 1935 what nihilism means for him, namely: 'to concern oneself only with beings in forgetfulness of Being' (*IM* 203/155). The overcoming [*Überwindung*] – or, as he puts it later, the

Denken?', in *VA* 2:16; *QB* 77; *ID* 31; 'Time and Being', in *On Time and Being*, translated by Joan Stambaugh (New York 1972), 1–24, 5; Brief an Richardson (1962), in William J. Richardson, SJ, *Heidegger: Through Phenomenology to Thought* (The Hague, 1963/1974), xxi.
[64] 'Was heisst Denken?', in *VA* 2:16.
[65] *QB* 101/*Wm* 249. See also *QB* 99/*Wm* 248, where Heidegger asks in typical fashion: 'Why is it . . . that "this Nothing" – that is, Being with regard to its essence [*Wesen*] – is not primarily given any thought?' Compare the 'Letter on Humanism', in *BW* 219, 223/*Wm* 169–70, 174.
[66] *Identity and Difference*, 39/28. Compare *QB* 35/*Wm* 214.

'getting over' [*Verwindung*][67] – of nihilism is then characterized as follows: 'To press the *inquiry* into Being expressly to the border of Nothing and to incorporate it [Nothing] into the question of Being' (*IM* 203/155). In this context Heidegger provides again in 1963 a highly informative self-interpretation in a letter to a Japanese colleague (as he had done in the 'letter' to Ernst Jünger in 1955 [*QB* 97/*Wm* 247]), which deals with the misunderstandings to which his major idea of 'Nothing' has been subject. He takes his characterization of the human being as 'place-holder [*Platzhalter*] of Nothing'[68] as a point of departure for the following clarification:

> That lecture ['What Is Metaphysics?' (1929)] which was translated into Japanese as early as 1930, was understood immediately in your country, in contrast to the nihilistic misunderstanding of what was said [about Nothing] which is prevalent to this day in Europe. The Nothing that is talked about there refers to that which in relation to what-is [*das Seiende*] is never any kind of being, and 'is' thus Nothing, but which nevertheless determines what-is as such and is thus called Being.[69]

A presentation of elements in Heidegger's texts can thus show that he thinks Nothing (with repeated elucidations) in such a way that, unlike in the West, it is immediately understood in Japan.[70] And yet a *non-Western* source for such thinking has presumably not been considered over there.[71]

This much is now clear: for Heidegger, the *topos* that corresponds to Being is Nothing, the primary topic of his thinking. The initial question

---

[67] *QB* 103, 109 /*Wm* 250, 253. [The English translation is highly misleading here, in so far as it renders *Verwindung* as the 'restoration' rather than 'getting over' of the forgetfulness of Being and nihilism.]

[68] 'What Is Metaphysics?', in *BW* 108/*Wm* 15. [Krell renders *Platzhalter des Nichts* as 'lieutenant of the nothing'.]

[69] 'Briefwechsel mit einem japanischen Kollegen' (1963), in *Begegnung: Zeitschrift für Literatur, Bildende Kunst, Musik und Wissenschaft* (1965):2–7, 6. [Also in *'JH'*.] In Heidegger's pseudo-dialogue (1959) – see Chapter 2 above – there is a corresponding passage that is, in parts, almost identical, and which is equally relevant to the question of influence: '– *I*: Emptiness is thus the same as Nothing, namely, that essential presencing [*jenes Wesende*] that we try to think as the Other to everything that is present or absent. – *J*: Certainly. That is why we in Japan immediately understood the lecture "What Is Metaphysics?" when it reached us by way of a translation in 1930 attempted by a Japanese student who was attending your lectures at the time. – We are still amazed that the Europeans could misinterpret the Nothing discussed in that lecture in a nihilistic way. For us emptiness [this is Heidegger's 'Japanese' speaking] is the highest name for that which you would like to speak of with the word "Being"' (*WL* 19/*US* 108–9).

[70] For the time being, it is irrelevant whether this contention rests simply on Heidegger's own opinion or else goes back to reliable and verifiable testimony from the Japanese themselves.

[71] Especially important for our investigation is *The Question of Being* ('Zur Seinsfrage') from 1955, which presumably originated during the same period as the 'Conversation', in so far as Heidegger makes significant mention of 'East Asian' language just before the end of that text (*QB* 107/Wm 252).

concerning the Being of beings has thereby received an answer, one that culminates in the formula: 'Being: Nothing: Same' ('SLT' 101). This Nothing is obviously no nugatory nothing: it is rather the 'Nothing of [*von*] Being [*Seyn*]',[72] an essential Nothing, a *real* Nothing. In other words: 'Even Nothing "belongs" for us to "Being"' (*IM* 85/64).

1.2   The East Asian way of thinking distinguishes itself in Daoism through the ancient insight, embodied in Chapter 2 of the *Laozi*, to the effect that *yu* (being) and *wu* (nothing) mutually produce one another (*xiang sheng*). Victor von Strauss translates the passage in question as follows: 'Being and non-being give birth to one another'; whereas Richard Wilhelm renders it as: 'Being and non-being engender one another'.[73] While Wilhelm in his commentary (which tends not to make precise distinctions) sometimes speaks of 'Being' [*Sein*] and now, with reference to *Laozi* 1, of 'being and non-being' [*Seiendes und Nichtseiendes*], stressing the 'unity' of the two (128; 42, 83), von Strauss speaks in his commentary on *Laozi* 2 of 'a correlative relationship between the two [*yu* and *wu*]' (174).[z] After emphasizing that one cannot talk of a temporal sequence here, 'nor simply of their simultaneity', he goes on to explain: 'Since one is, or comes to be, only through the other, the poet can say that being and non-being [*Sein und Nichtsein*] mutually produce, engender, or give birth to one another' (175).

Chapter 40 of the *Laozi* goes on to elaborate the idea that everything [*alles Seiende*] in the world, or all things [*wan wu*] originate [*sheng*] from being [*yu*], and that being [*yu*] originates [*sheng*] from nothing [*wu*]. Von Strauss translates: 'All beings originate from being, / Being originates from non-being'.[74a] In other words: 'Being shows itself in Nothing [*am Nichts*], but also vice versa; the two constantly come to expression reciprocally, one in the other [*am Anderen*]'.[75]

---

[72] *SZ* (*GA* 2) 10, footnote a. [This footnote, which is not in the Niemeyer edition, reads: 'Da-sein: als Hineingehaltenheit in das Nichts von Seyn, als Verhältnis gehalten'.] Compare von Herrmann, *Hermeneutische Phänomenologie des Daseins*, 74, who notes that the 'y'-spelling indicates 'that Being . . . is here being thought in the way of being [*Wesen*] (and holding sway [*Walten*]) that is proper to it'.

[73] Von Strauss, *Lao-Tse* 58 [1870: 10]; Richard Wilhelm, *Laotse, Tao te king. Das Buch des Alten vom Sinn und Leben* (Düsseldorf/Cologne 1957, 1972), 42 [Jena 1911, 4].

[74] 'Alle Wesen entstehen aus dem Sein, / Das Sein entsteht aus dem Nichtsein' (von Strauss, *Lao-Tse* 111; see also 302f [1870: 186, 187f]). Compare Wilhelm on *Laozi* 40. The influential Chinese commentary of Wang Bi (226–49) contains the following explanation: 'All things in the world came from being, and the origin of being is based on non-being. To have being in total, it is necessary to return to non-being' (*Commentary on the Lao Tzu by Wang Pi*, translated by Ariane Rump [Honolulu 1979], 123; with reference to Wing-tsit Chan, the translator of this passage). On *Laozi* 40, compare Ch'en Ku-Ying, *Lao Tzu: Text, Notes and Comments*, translated and adapted by Rhett Y. W. Young and Roger T. Ames (San Francisco 1977): 'The term "Being" [*yu*] should not be confused with the Parmenidian concept of "Being" – for Parmenides, there is one, unchanging, unmoving, real existence, and this he calls "Being". For him, there is no "Non-Being" [*wu*]' (201–3, 202). Compare also the comments and the reference in note 61 above.

This kind of correspondence between being and nothing is character-istic of the basic insights of East Asian doctrines concerning *dao*. This perspective was taken over by Zen Buddhism in the Mahāyāna tradition, synthesized with similar insights from early Buddhism, and then devel-oped further. This is clear from two Zen texts that are translated in the collection by Ōhazama Shūei, which in all probability – almost certainly – Heidegger knew well and appreciated for deepening and enriching his knowledge of the field.[76] A passage in the *Shinjin-mei* ['The Seal of Faith'] reads: 'Being is none other than nothing, / nothing is none other than being' (70). And in the *Shōdō-ka* ['Hymn on the Experience of the Way']: 'Nothing is everything, and / everything is nothing brought to completion' (73; cf. 84).[b]

Finally, we find in a text from 1939 by Nishida Kitarō, who can be regarded as the pioneer of comparative philosophy from the East–West perspective, the easily remembered formula: 'Being is nothing, nothing is being'.[77] Fifteen years after the publication of Nishida's article in German, Tezuka elucidates, in response to a pointed question of Heidegger's, the (classic) Zen Buddhist way of thinking mentioned earlier,[78] and on which Heidegger appears to play adroitly in his 'Conversation'.[79c]

1.3 Let us now juxtapose the relevant textual excerpts. First:

> . . . *that one is only through the other* . . . (*Laozi* 2, von Strauss commen-tary).

The Other to it [Being] is simply Nothing (Heidegger, *IM* 79/60).

---

[75] Compare Ellen Marie Chen, 'The Origin and Development of Being (*Yu*) from Non-Being (*Wu*) in the *Tao Te Ching*', *International Philosophical Quarterly* 13 (1973):403–17, 412ff; Charles Wei-Hsun Fu, 'Creative Hermeneutics: Taoist Metaphysics and Heidegger', *Journal of Chinese Philosophy* 3 (1976):115–43, 131–4; and Cho, *Bewusstein und Natursein*, 181f.

[76] Schüej Ōhasama, *Zen: Der lebendige Buddhismus in Japan*, edited by August Faust (Gotha/Stuttgart 1925). See above Chapter 1, note 4. [This book also contains a foreword by Rudolf Otto, whose work in this context must have played a role for Heidegger that should not be overlooked.]

[77] Kitarō Nishida, 'Die morgenländischen und abendländischen Kulturformen in alter Zeit vom metaphysischen Standpunkt aus gesehen' ['Oriental and occidental forms of culture in antiquity, seen from the metaphysical standpoint'], *Abhandlungen der preussischen Akademie der Wissenschaften* 19 (Berlin 1939):12. A comparison between Nishida's ideas about time and those elaborated by Heidegger in 'Zeit und Sein' would be a worthwhile enterprise.

[78] Tezuka employs (61f below) the famous formulation, now almost a proverb in Japan, from the *Prajñā-pāramitā-hṛdaya-sūtra*, the Daoist overtones of which are unmistakable. In this context, one must bear in mind the important mediating role of Chinese Daoism in the appropriation and translation of the Indian teachings of the Buddha.

Compare in this context the remarkable work by Nishitani Keiji, *Religion and Nothingness*, translated by Jan Van Bragt (Berkeley/London 1982), 97, 107, as well as Hans Waldenfels, *Absolute Nothingness: Foundations for a Buddhist–Christian Dialogue*, translated by James W. Heisig (New York 1980), a notable work in comparative religion that treats our present topic also with respect to the relations between Nishitani's and Heidegger's thinking (77–9).

[79] See the 'Conversation', in *WL* 19/*US* 108 (also footnote 69 above) in connection with 14–15/102, 41/137; and compare **2.4** above.

Being and Nothing are not given beside one another. Each uses itself on behalf of the other ... (*QB* 97/*Wm* 247).[d]

Second:

Being is none other than nothing, / Nothing is none other than being.[80]

Nothing as 'Being' (Heidegger, 'WM?' [*GA* 9] 106, note b).

Nothing and Being the Same ('WM?' [*GA* 9] 115, note c).

Being: Nothing: Same ('SLT' 101).[e]

These passages juxtaposed in this way, while of course needing to be understood in context, allow hardly any doubt to remain that in Heidegger's non-Western understanding of 'Nothing' ('Being'), which is elaborated clearly and distinctly in his later texts (see **1.1**), and in the light of which he wants to have his earlier texts just as clearly understood, he is indebted to Daoist and Zen Buddhist ways of thinking.[81] We have good grounds, then, for supposing that Heidegger elaborated (sometimes verbatim) these kinds of correspondence with the help of the texts named above, with which he was familiar (see Chapter 1), and integrated them into his work.

2.1 A similar situation appears to obtain with respect to Heidegger's understanding and presentation of the problematic of the *thing*, which he deals with in several different texts. A textual comparison brings to light a similarity between the sentence patterns Heidegger employs with respect to the characterization of Being in *Being and Time* and the characterization of the thing in the so-called 'thing lecture-course' from 1935 to 1936.[82] In the Western philosophical tradition, things (in the narrower

---

[80] *Shinjin-mei* in the translation of Ōhazama (70); compare Nishida, 'Die morgenländischen und abendländischen Kulturformen' 12.

[81] Taking a cue from Martin Buber in his edition of the *Zhuangzi*, one could say that Heidegger in the West overcomes 'the traditional wisdom through the teaching of "non-being" [*Nichtsein*]' just as Laozi did in China (Buber, *Chinese Tales* 87/92 [subsequent references to Buber's *Zhuangzi* will be made to the page numbers of the English translation and German original respectively]). Since Heidegger occasionally recited passages from Buber's *Zhuangzi*, one can assume that he was familiar with this passage.

  Already Schelling, whose work Heidegger knew well, sums up the *Laozi*'s understanding of *dao* as follows: 'The great art or wisdom of life is precisely to maintain this pure ability that is at the same time nothing [*Nichts*] and everything. The entire *Dao de jing* is concerned to show, through various combinations of pregnant expressions, the great and insuperable power of non-being [*des nicht Seyenden*]' (F. W. J. von Schelling, 'Philosophie der Mythologie', in *Ausgewählte Schriften* [Frankfurt a.M. 1985], 6/2:576). This reference is by no means irrelevant to our investigation.

[82] See *SZ* 6 and *What is a Thing?* [*WT?*], translated by W. B. Barton and Vera Deutsch (Chicago 1967), 8–10, cf. 47/*Die Frage nach dem Ding* [*FD*] (Tübingen 1962), 6–7, cf. 36. [Further references within the body of the text will be made by the abbreviation '*WT?*' and followed by the page numbers of the English and German editions repectively.] The lecture 'The Thing' of 1950 will be discussed in the next section (**2.2**).

sense) are understood as all non-human entities.[83] Heidegger himself offers a (broader) characterization when he writes: 'In the language of philosophy things in themselves and things that appear, everything [*alles Seiende*] that in any way is, is called a thing.'[84f]

The real question, which leads pointedly into the elucidation of 'the being' [*Wesen*] of things, is originally posed in the Freiburg lecture from the winter semester 1935/6 that was given under the title 'Basic Questions of Metaphysics' and published in 1962 as *The Question of the Thing: On Kant's Doctrine of Transcendental Principles* [title of the English translation: *What is a Thing?*]. The appropriate answer must be sought (and understood), according to Heidegger, in the context of 'the changing fundamental position within the relation to beings', as 'the task of an entire age'.[85] This means, for Heidegger, giving up the idea that Plato, Aristotle, and 'all subsequent thinkers' – one would have to add, in the Western philosophical tradition – have thought 'the being [*Wesen*] of the thing' adequately.[86]

Heidegger nevertheless attempts with his elucidation a new beginning from an unaccustomed perspective, one that can find an appropriate starting-point only outside Western philosophical thinking. 'The question of the thing comes from its origin into motion [*Bewegung*] again' (*WT?* 48/36). His (non-Western) answer corresponds almost verbatim to the following expression:

What gives things their thingness is not itself a thing (*Zhuangzi*, 22).[87]

And according to Heidegger:

[The] thingness of the thing ... cannot itself be a thing again (*WT?* 9/7, cf. 36).

Compare with the well-known formulation in *Being and Time*:

The Being of beings 'is' not itself a being (*SZ* 6).[g]

In both these cases Heidegger's answer (congruent with the connections articulated above) runs parallel to what he says about Nothing (or emptiness: see next section),[88] as in the lecture on the thing: 'The

[83] Compare von Herrmann, *Hermeneutische Phänomenologie des Daseins*, 67.
[84] 'The Origin of the Work of Art', in *PLT* 21. Compare *WT?* 5–7, where Heidegger distinguishes the narrower, broader, and broadest senses; also 'The Nature of Language', in *WL* 62.
[85] *WT?* 50/38 [translation modified]; see also 51/39f.
[86] 'The Thing', in *PLT* 168/'Das Ding', in *VA* 2:40; compare 'The Origin of the Work of Art', in *PLT* 32, 39/*Hw* 21, 28.
[87] Translation by Richard Wilhelm: *Dschuang Dsï [Chuang Tzu]. Das wahre Buch vom südlichen Blütenland* (Jena 1912), 167; (Düsseldorf/Cologne 1972), 233f.
[88] In 'The Origin of the Work of Art' (also 1935, 1936) Heidegger remarks, significantly: 'That the thingness of the thing is especially difficult to put into words, and seldom can be, is attested to by the history of its interpretations indicated above. This history is congruent with the fate [*Schicksal*] in accordance with which Western [!] thinking has hitherto thought the Being of beings' (*PLT* 32/*Hw* 21). Nothing more need be said.

thingness [*Dingheit*] [of the thing] must be something unconditioned [*Un-bedingtes*]' (*WT?* 9/7). No different conclusion could be reached with the *Zhuangzi*, if we think through to the end the idea in it that we cited above.[89h]

It is now clear that Heidegger's elucidation of the thing-problematic corresponds in substance to that presented in section **1.3** above. It will thus have become equally clear where Heidegger has sought and found the starting-point for his new beginning.

2.2   It is possible to show the influence of East Asian ways of thinking in another, similar context: namely, in the lecture 'The Thing' from 1950. A passage from Chapter 11 of the *Laozi* reads, in Wilhelm's translation: 'The work of pitchers consists in their nothingness [Nichts, *wu*]' (51). Von Strauss translates: 'The use of the container [*Gefäss*] accords with its non-being [*Nicht-sein*]' (68; cf. 204–6).[i] The first part of the lecture on the thing engages this issue in several passages. Heidegger speaks of a jug, saying: 'The jug is a thing as container [*Gefäss*]'.[90] Also: 'The thingly character [*Dinghafte*] of the thing, however, does not consist in its being a repre-sented object, nor can it be determined at all in terms of the objectness of the object' (*PLT* 167/*VA* 2:39).

The question of the thingly character [*Dinghaftigkeit*] of the thing had been raised earlier (1935 and 1936) in 'The Origin of the Work of Art' in connection with the lecture course on 'The Thing'.[91] In the later lecture Heidegger continues the elucidation begun in the mid-1930s by following *Laozi* 11, in so far as he paraphrases as follows: 'The thingly character of the container [*Gefäss*] does not in any way consist in the material of which it is made, but rather in the emptiness [*Leere*] that does the containing [*fasst*]'.[92] Recall that in the 'Conversation' it is said that 'emptiness is . . . the same as Nothing' (*WL* 19/*US* 108).

If in a marginal note in *Being and Time* Heidegger remarks on the topic 'Nothing of Being [*Seyn*]' (*SZ* [*GA*] 10a), so in a similar context, estab-lishing as it were the connection between *Being and Time* and his later philosophy, he speaks of the 'emptiness of Being . . . [which] is never to

---

[89] Compare the translation of *Zhuangzi* 22 in the Buber edition (75/76), and also this rendering by Hans O. H. Stange, *Tschuang-Tse. Dichtung und Weisheit* (Leipzig 1936), 69: 'That which first makes things things does not itself have the delimitation of a thing.' A literal translation would read: 'That which things things has with respect to things no limit.' – thus 'Nothing' or 'emptiness'.

[90] 'The Thing', in *PLT*, 168/*VA* 2:40.

[91] 'The Origin of the Work of Art', in *PLT* 20–2/*Hw* 11–12.

[92] 'The Thing', in *PLT* 169/*VA* 2:41. Compare *Laozi* 11, and especially the commentary by von Strauss (205). See also Cho on this topic, who writes, with great circumspection that nevertheless makes the point in question perfectly clear: 'Heidegger's description of the "emptiness" of the container seems to echo, both in the choice of motif as well as in the choice of words, on Laozi's lines in Chapter 11 of the *Dao de jing*' (*Bewusstsein und Natursein*, 302; also 92). For a similar judgement see Parkes, 'Thoughts on the Way' (*HAT* 120f, 142f).

be filled by the plenitude of beings'.[93] Speaking again (in 1969) of 'Being', he remarks comprehensibly and conclusively 'that Being was never thought *as* Being by the Greeks or even brought into question' ('SLT' 105). Thus, for Heidegger the return to Greek thinking makes sense only when combined with the return to the *original* reposing of the question of the *Being* of beings ('SLT' 105), that is – to amplify a little[94] – only when *Being* as the Same of Being and Nothing is thereby brought *through poetic thinking* [*denkend-dichtend*] (to stay with Heidegger's way of speaking) on to the *way*. At any rate, we must be prepared for what Heidegger recognized as early as 1935: 'True talk about Nothing always remains uncommon' (*IM* 26/20). In the West, at least, so far.

3 Let us now turn to another *topos* that Heidegger often treats in his texts, and which he apparently employs in the contexts here articulated for the purpose of illustrating his thinking. From *Being and Time* on, he uses in appropriate contexts the word 'clearing' [*Lichtung*] in his elucidations of Being and Nothing. A selection of six relevant texts will help clarify his use of this key term. His aim is obviously to present a matter that plays a role in connection with the word 'nothing' in ancient Chinese thought, but in a pictographic constellation, the meaning of which is hardly even thought of any more today.

As far as *Being and Time* is concerned, it remains an open question whether Heidegger is providing an *explanation* or a *reinterpretation* when he adds the marginal note, '*Alētheia* – Openness – clearing, light, shining'.[95j] This remark may indicate that he later uses the word 'clearing' in a distinctive sense, in the sense of unconcealedness, openness, the Open. By comparison with *Being and Time*, the point is made more clearly in the essay on the work of art, where Heidegger offers the following formulation that is significant [*wegweisend*] for his many subsequent elaborations: 'In the midst of beings as a whole there is [*west*] an open place. There is a clearing. This clearing is, thought from the side of beings, more 'being' [*seiender*] than beings. ... The luminous [*lichtend*] middle itself encircles like Nothing ... all that is [*alles Seiende*]' (*PLT* 53/41).[k]

---

[93] 'Overcoming Metaphysics', in *The End of Philosophy*, translated by Joan Stambaugh (New York 1973), 107 ['Überwindung der Metaphysik', in *VA* 1:87]. In his customary 'References' at the end of the volume Heidegger says the following about 'Overcoming Metaphysics' (published in 1954): 'The text gives sketches for the overcoming of metaphysics [compare *QB* 100ff/250f] from 1936 to 1946' (*VA* 1:119). This text, which is divided into twenty-eight small sections, thus constitutes a kind of bridge between his early and late work, which he understands as a 'way of thinking, poetizing building/cultivation [*dichtenden Bauens*]' (according to the end of the text, p. 110/91).

[94] Heidegger writes in 1963, interpreting himself, to his Japanese colleague Kojima Takehiko: 'The step back does not mean that thinking flees back to bygone ages, and above all not [!] a reanimation of the beginning of Western philosophy' ('Briefwechsel mit einem japanischen Kollegen', 6/*JH* 224). Heidegger published this letter in 1965, a year before his three telling propositions in the *Der Spiegel* interview (see above, **1.2.3**).

Later in the essay Heidegger writes: 'Self-concealing Being [is] illuminated [*gelichtet*]' (*PLT* 56/44). Turned around, this amounts to saying that *unconcealed Nothing is nihilated*. In a later text, from 1943, we find the expression, now easier to understand, 'The shining of the clearing [that is: of Nothing] is in itself simultaneously a self-veiling – and is in this sense what is darkest'.[96]

It is surprising perhaps, and yet for us still understandable and consonant with his other remarks, that Heidegger eventually says in one of his last texts (1964): 'But philosophy knows nothing of the clearing. Philosophy certainly speaks of the light [*Licht*] of reason, but does not pay attention to the clearing [*Lichtung*] of Being'.[97]

How does Heidegger arrive at this apparent identification of the clearing with Nothing, which is not to be found in the Western philosophical tradition? One might certainly think of the medieval metaphysics of light, and yet sufficient points of contact are hardly to be found there. But things look different in the realm of Chinese language. There we find, in the interpretation of the Chinese graph [written character] for 'nothing', namely *wu*, a rich starting-point for the identification of the clearing and Nothing: *wu* refers to a place that was originally covered in luxuriant vegetation, as in a thicket in a wood, but where trees have been felled so that there is now an open space, a clearing. *Wu* thus means '*there, where there is nothing*', a place where formerly there were trees.[98] A consonant interpretation is given by León Wieger in his book *Chinese Characters*, which has gone through many editions since 1915:

---

[95] *SZ* (*GA* 2), 177a; compare *SZ* 350, 170. See also 'On the Essence of Truth', in *BW* 140; and 'Der Weg zur Sprache', in *GA* 12:234a, b [notes absent from the English translation, 'The Way to Language', in *WL*].

[96] 'Aletheia', in *Early Greek Thinking*, 123 [*VA* 3:77–8]. Heidegger's 'plays' with tautologies, which become more frequent after around 1946 and are often confusing at first, can be elucidated by an example from the 'Letter on Humanism'. There he writes: 'But the clearing itself is Being' (*BW* 211/*Wm* 163); and a few paragraphs later: 'The self-giving into the Open together with this very Open is Being itself' (214/165). From this it follows that the clearing itself is the self-giving into the Open (into emptiness, into Nothing). Compare also *BW* 228–9/*Wm* 180. In this text, as Heidegger himself remarks, he resumes a line of thinking begun in 1936 that 'still speaks in the language of metaphysics, and does so wittingly', and which leaves 'the other language' in the background (footnote to the title of the essay in the version reprinted in *GA* 9:313). How 'the other language' gleams forth from the background is intimated by a passage close to the end of the 'Letter': 'This thinking is, insofar as it is, memorial thinking [*Andenken*] of Being and nothing besides. Belonging [*gehörig*] to Being, because thrown by Being into the preservation [*Wahrnis*] of its truth and claimed for this preservation, it thinks Being. Such thinking has no result. It has no effect. It is adequate to its being [*Wesen*] in that it is' (*BW* 236/*Wm* 188). Heidegger wrote this text to Jean Beaufret in Paris several weeks after his attempts at translating the *Laozi* with Paul Hsiao, and published it with some expansions in 1947.

[97] 'The End of Philosophy and the Task of Thinking', in *BW* 386. Compare the discussion of 'Nothing of Being' [*Nichts von Seyn*] in section **1.1** above.

[98] See Morohashi Tetsuji, *Dai kan-wa jiten* [Chinese–Japanese dictionary], 13 vols (Tokyo 1986), entry no. 19113, in conjunction with 49188, 15783, 15514. It is, of course, highly unlikely that Heidegger could have drawn from this source, even though this monumental work began to be published in 1955.

A multitude ... of men, acting upon a forest, felling the trees, clearing of wood a tract of land. In the old form [the graph] stated that the wood had vanished. Hence ... the general abstract notions of vanishing, defect, want, negation.[99]

A passage of Heidegger's from the 1960s reads correspondingly as follows:

To clear [*lichten*] something means: to make something light, free and open; for example, to make a place in the woods free of trees. The open space that results is the clearing [*Lichtung*].[100]

Corresponding to the assimilation described above, this means that Heidegger can again use instead of 'Nothing' the word 'clearing' in its extended sense and insert it into the appropriate place in his text. But in 'The End of Philosophy' he uses another word, though with a corresponding meaning and in consonance with the passage cited above from the essay on the work of art (*PLT* 53/41): 'The clearing is the Open [Nothing] for all presencing and being absent' (*BW* 384/*SD* 72). The elaborations that follow underscore through paraphrase the presented topic. The 'clearing of Being' is thus *the same* as the 'Nothing of Being [*Seyn*]'.[101]

The similarity between the cited passages from Heidegger and Wieger is difficult to overlook.[102] Nevertheless, there remains *in this case* a doubt as to whether Heidegger actually drew on Wieger's text in elaborating his concept for the assimilation of Nothing and clearing. It is by no means improbable that Wieger's book (like those of Martin Buber and Richard Wilhelm – both theologians as were many other scholars of that era and earlier to whom we are indebted for mediating East Asian thought) was available since 1915 in the libraries of theological seminaries (more so than of philosophy departments) and that Heidegger could thus have come across a copy. Even so, one must bear in mind that he could have assimilated and elaborated 'Nothing' and 'clearing' and worked with it simply

[99] León Wieger, SJ, *Chinese Characters. Their Origin, Etymology, History, Classification and Signification: A Thorough Study from Chinese Documents*, translated by L. Davrout, SJ; reprint (New York 1965), 36.
[100] 'The End of Philosophy', in *BW* 384/*SD* 72. [Again, the English translation has 'to open' for *lichten*, 'to clear'.]
[101] 'The End of Philosophy', in *BW* 386/*SD* 73; *SZ* 10a. Taking – prompted by Heidegger himself – 'clearing' in the sense of 'Nothing' helps us to understand the following passages, which recapitulate familiar themes with only slight variations: 'Clearing [*Lichten*] is thus more than merely illuminating, and also more than uncovering. Clearing is the musing-gathering bringing forth into the open, the granting [*Gewähren*] of presencing [Being]' ('Aletheia', in *EGT* 118/*VA* 3:72). And also: 'The clearing [Nothing] not only illuminates what is present [beings], but it gathers and shelters it in advance into presencing [Being]' ('Aletheia', 120/74).
[102] Compare Michael Heim, 'A Philosophy of Comparison: Heidegger and Lao Tzu', in *Journal of Chinese Philosophy* 11 (1984):307–35, 316 (also with reference to other texts and contexts); and Chang Chung-yuan, in *EMH* 68. (Chang identifies *Lichtung* with *ming*, with Heidegger's assent. But there is surely a misunderstanding here, in so far as *ming* catches an incidental aspect of *Lichtung* which is of minor concern to Heidegger by comparison with *wu* [Nothing].)

on the basis of his acquaintance with East Asian thought (and explanations on the part of his East Asian interlocutors) in conjunction with all the possible ways of understanding the German word *Lichtung* (one thinks, for example, of the word *Waldblösse* [a gap in the forest through which light can enter]). In this case, then, one would have to regard the similarity to the passage from Wieger as merely fortuitous.

4 *Dao*: way and saying

1 Let us now pursue the question of the influence on Heidegger of Daoist ideas with respect to another key term of his, namely 'Saying' [*Sage*].^m Two texts in particular suggest themselves in this connection, 'The Nature [*Wesen*] of Language' (1957, 1958) and 'The Way to Language' (1959), both of which belong to Heidegger's so-called late philosophy.[103] In the text of the earlier lecture (see *GA* 12:260) Heidegger mentions the word *dao* five times and concludes a most informative paragraph with the words 'All is way' [*Alles ist Weg*] (*WL* 92/*US* 198). The second text, which was delivered and published a little later, can be understood as a valuable amplification of the first. Moreover, it will strike the careful reader that these two texts are indirectly related and mutually illuminate one another, and thereby become more comprehensible.

As in the previous chapter, we shall try to interpret the contours of Heidegger's thinking by remaining within his text itself, so as to contribute to the solution of the enigma presented by these two later essays. We must here again expect Heidegger's subtle paraphrasing technique to come to *expression*, and also that we shall have to deal with a number of concealed allusions to internal textual contexts. Having already become aware of such factors (see Chapters 2 and 3), we shall be able to follow the course of his thinking more easily and complement it with respect to its meaning where necessary by referring to other texts.

Ultimately, a deeper understanding can be attained, and the insights gained here elaborated, only by way of a comprehensive and detailed exegesis of both texts, which cannot be attempted here. Our investigation concentrates primarily on answering the question of influence posed at the beginning, and will thus have to tolerate gaps in the interpretation.

As mentioned earlier, Heidegger ponders in the texts under discussion the *topos* 'Saying', which becomes a key term for him on the *way* to language. The nature of language, the 'essential totality of language' [*das Sprachwesen im Ganzen*], he calls 'Saying' (*WL* 123/*US* 253). 'The distinctive feature of language [*Sprachwesen*]', however, 'is concealed [*verbirgt*

---

[103] In *WL* 57–108, 111–36/*US* 157–216, 239–68.

sich] in the Way' (126/257). The converse of this formulation follows a few pages later: 'Within this Way, which belongs to the essence of language, is concealed the distinctive feature of language' (129/260–1).

A remark in the earlier text ('On the Nature of Language') that is striking simply on account of its content comes to play a key role here. One should note in particular the phrase 'is concealed', which Heidegger employs again in these three passages, and surely not fortuitously: 'Perhaps there is concealed in the word "Way", *dao*, the mystery of all mysteries of thinking Saying, if we let these names revert to *that which is unspoken* in them and are capable of this letting' (92/198; emphasis added).[n] Heidegger speaks then, to emphasize once again, of 'the mystery of all mysteries of thinking Saying'. This sentence is surely clear enough. He then ends the paragraph with the words 'All is way [*dao*]'.

In this context another very important *topos*, that of 'Appropriation' [*Ereignis*], plays an important role, to which we shall return later.[o] It is sufficient for now to say that these formulations of Heidegger's are obviously intended to assimilate 'Way' and 'Saying' – something that can be easily shown in a series of formulations. For example: 'In language as Saying there holds sway something like a Way' (126/256). Or: 'The Way . . . as Saying is language as Saying' (126/257). To abbreviate, this means simply, in consonance with 'All is Way': Way is Saying, and vice versa, Saying is Way (*dao*). We will come across similar assimilations later.

At the beginning of the second lecture ['The Nature of Language'] Heidegger proposes giving thought to the 'Way' (74/178). He then makes a transition from the verbs 'think' [*denken*] and 'poetize' [*dichten*],[p] which always play an important role for him, to the word 'Saying' (83f/188f). Thus: 'Saying is the same element for composing and for thinking' (84/189); it is related to the very being of language (76/180). And through the multiply resonant and, for Heidegger, determinative closeness of poetizing and thinking, he arrives at another important *topos* – namely 'Nearness' [*Nähe*]. He connects this with the *topos* 'Saying' in the following formulation: 'But the nearness that brings poetizing and thinking close to one another we call Saying' (93/199–200). He then simply identifies, having prepared the ground in this way, 'Nearness' and 'Saying' (95/202). Finally, by way of clarification: 'Quiet consideration lets one see to what extent Nearness and Saying as the essential element [*das Wesende*] of language are the same' (107/214). In this way, Heidegger step by step approaches the formula: 'Way equals Saying equals Nearness'. With this last term he clearly links (his own) poetizing and thinking to the nearness of *dao*.

By means of a further formulation already mentioned, Heidegger arrives at yet another identification of 'Way' and 'Saying'. He achieves this by adducing the key word 'Appropriation', and by emphasizing in turn what is (according to him) an ancient word: '*The motive force in the showing of Saying is 'propriating'* [Eignen]' (127/258).[q] This means: propriating moves itself in the showing of Saying; and this then becomes, through two further moves of thought, 'Appropriating' [*Ereignen*].

We shall go more fully into the meaning of the word 'Appropriation' in an interpretation of the longer passage at the centre of which this key word stands. For now, these two statements – 'The Way is appropriating [*ereignend*]' (129/261) and 'Appropriation is saying [*sagend*]' (131/263) – will suffice to show again how Heidegger identifies 'Way' and 'Saying'. Walter Uhsadel remarked this identification as early as 1961.[104]

2 While the identification of 'Way' and 'Saying', or the relating of 'Saying' to 'Way', is admittedly not an everyday affair from the East Asian perspective, nor something immediately comprehensible to everyone, it is by no means merely arbitrary. The Chinese word *dao*, which Heidegger mentions several times in this context (92/198), can be lexically grasped also by the verb 'say', which is in certain contexts the appropriate translation.[105r] The first chapter of the *Laozi* provides a good example of this, especially since Heidegger was surely acquainted with this chapter and the interpretation of it in the Richard Wilhelm translation (1911), which discusses these connections [between *dao* and saying].[106s]

Heidegger's way of writing the name *Laozi*, which he always transcribes as 'Laotse', clearly derives from Wilhelm or from Hsiao, who seems to have followed Wilhelm's romanization.[107] All the other translations of the *Laozi* then extant use a different romanization. And Hsiao must surely have elaborated on Wilhelm with clarifying explanations in the course of the collaboration with Heidegger on the *Laozi* translation in 1946.

Finally, there is the obvious consideration that Heidegger learned from Buber's edition of the *Zhuangzi*. The semantic correspondences and resonances of various kinds are all too clear, quite apart from the indication (here too) of the relations of *dao* to Way and speech (Saying).[108] To demonstrate these correspondences we shall adduce verbatim three passages from Buber's afterword and two from the translation.

---

[104] 'The book is heavily loaded with such strange identifications. The goal is apparently to use etymology and these kinds of definitions [adduced by Uhsadel] to arrive at the identification of the most important phenomena of language with the idea of "Way"' (Walter Uhsadel, 'Review [of *US*]', 219).

[105] See Rüdenberg/Stange, *Chinesisch-Deutsches Wörterbuch*, Hamburg: 1924, 1963, no. 6062. For further references to *dao* as 'saying', see Morohashi, *Dai kan-wa jiten*, no. 39010, II.1. [Also H. A. Giles, *A Chinese–English Dictionary* (1892, 1972) no. 10.780; and *Mathews' Chinese–English Dictionary* (1931, 1972), no. 6136d.]

[106] Wilhelm, *Laotse: Tao te king*, 25 [1911, xv]. The question of whether other relationships of a textual nature are operative in Heidegger's thinking on this topic would require further detailed exegeses. Compare Johannes Lohmann, 'Der Sophismus des Kung-Sun Lung (zur ontologischen Amphibolie des Chinesischen)', in *Lexis* 2 (1949):3–11, 6. This author, an interlocutor of Heidegger's who was competent in matters of Chinese language, also calls attention to the fact that *dao* means 'say' as well as 'Way'.

[107] Hsiao, 'Laotse und die Technik', 72–4.

[108] See Buber, *Tschuang-Tse* 'Afterword', 92–3/'Nachwort', 100.

The word *dao* means way, path: but since it also has the meaning of speech [*Rede*], it has sometimes been rendered by 'Logos'. In Laozi and his disciples, where it has always been developed metaphorically, it is associated with the first of these meanings. And yet its linguistic atmosphere is actually related to that of the Heraclitean *Logos* (100).

Dao does not mean any kind of world-explanation, but rather that the entire meaning of Being [*Sinn des Seins*!] rests in the unity of true life, is experienced only in that unity, and that it *is* precisely this unity taken as the Absolute. If one wants to look away from the unity of true life and contemplate what 'underlies' it, there is nothing left but the unknowable, of which no more can be said than that it is unknowable (101).

Dao appears ... as the primordial indivisibility ... as the 'spirit of the valley' that supports everything' (105–6).

Does Heidegger not revert to this, with a corresponding meaning, when he offers the following formulation?

Dao could thus be the Way that moves everything [*der alles be-wëgende Weg*], that from which we might first be able to think what reason, spirit, meaning, Logos authentically – from their own being – want to say. Perhaps there is concealed in the word 'Way', *dao*, the mystery of all mysteries of thinking Saying, if we let these names return to that which is unspoken in them and are capable of this letting. ... [M]ethods ... are simply the effluents of an enormous underground river, of the Way that moves everything and rushes everything onto its way. All is Way (92/198).

Let us now consolidate by adducing the two passages of translation from the Buber edition of the *Zhuangzi*. First: 'The being [*Wesen*] of perfect *dao* is deeply hidden; its reaches lose themselves in the dark' (43). Second: 'Thus is perfect *dao*. And thus is also the archetypal Word [thus also Saying]' (76). Compare the note Heidegger appended near the end of 'The Way to Language' in the *Gesamtausgabe* ['Word – Saying that announces].[t]

The attentive reader will presumably be able to ascertain a whole series of further similarities without much difficulty, especially if one juxtaposes these passages and many others in the Buber edition with Heidegger's eloquent [*wortgewandten*] and 'word-changing' [*Worte wandelnden*] elucidations.[109]

Heidegger's identification of 'Way' and 'Saying' therefore most likely has its source in texts concerning doctrines of *dao* in German translations

---

[109] See, for example, 'The Way to Language' (*WL* 84/*US* 189, 86f/192f, 91–4/197–200) and 'The Nature of Language' (122–3/253, 130/261).

and commentaries. On this premise, together with a consideration of what was presented in Chapter 3 above, his further elucidations of the 'nature of language' and the 'way to language', in conjunction, of course, with his own explanatory interpretations, become more easily comprehensible and reconstructable. In this way, their enigmatic nature may be to a great extent resolved[110] – or at least brought closer to resolution by appropriate transpositions, without thereby losing the 'message' intended by the author or 'messenger' ('Conversation' 54/155). We might thereby discover what Heidegger means when, a few years before his texts on language, he makes the anticipatory remark: 'The polysemous nature [*Mehrdeutigkeit*] of Saying by no means consists in a mere accumulation of arbitrary meanings. It lies in a play that, the more richly it unfolds, the more rigorously it remains within a hidden rule'.[111]

3.1 In dealing with the two main topics of Daoist thought, *wu* (Nothing) and *dao*, and with the latter term's ambiguity between 'Way' and 'Saying' that inspires Heidegger's thinking, his programme of textual appropriation employing encoded phrases becomes apparent at a significant level.

Heidegger connects Saying, which has 'no Being', with an 'illumining-concealing freeing' of world, or with an illumining-veiling extending of world.[112] He thus implicitly associates (in the spirit of Daoist doctrine) 'Way' (*dao*) with region [*Gegend*] as the freeing 'clearing [Nothing], in which what is illumined reaches the Open [*das Freie*, Nothing] together with what conceals itself [Being]' (91/197). With respect to the identifications discussed in Chapter 3 – especially the formulation 'Being: Nothing: Same' along with all the subsequent characteristic identifications such as those of 'clearing', 'the Open' [*das Offene*], 'Openness' [*das Freie*] with *Nothing*, and 'hiddenness', 'being-veiled', and 'forgottenness' with *Being* – all further possible identifications (including their appropriate combinations) are understandable on the model of *dao* (Way/Saying), *wu* (Nothing), and *yu* (Being), quite in Heidegger's sense, who must have elaborated them according to such formulas. Saying or *Sage* (*dao*), then, naturally has no Being.

[110] These texts of Heidegger's ultimately remained enigmatic even for Uhsadel. In his critical but objective review, Uhsadel remarks that Heidegger's understanding of language as monological 'stands in clear contrast to the biblical view' (220), which sees it as dialogical. Heidegger neither refers to language as a way from one human being to another, nor does he open up through language a 'perspective on the dialogue between God and the human being'. He thus speaks 'of language as if it were a creature, but of the human being as if it were the work or instrument of language'; theologically speaking, Heidegger's talk of language would be 'a deification of language'. Uhsadel concludes his review with the words: 'We need to mention one last concern: that this philosophy may one day reveal itself in theology as the most incisive attack on Christian faith since Nietzsche – by which time it may be too late' (221).
[111] *QB* 105/*Wm* 251. Compare also the by no means superfluous elucidations of 'play' and 'word-play' in *WCT?*, 118f [*Was heisst Denken?* 83f].

We can see now that we must constantly be prepared for an encoding employment of words similar in meaning in the context of Heideggerian assimilations if we are not to lose the significant thread that runs throughout his texts. For, as Heidegger himself says, 'All is Way' (*WL* 92/*US* 198) – an idea he takes up in numerous variations in both his essays on language. For example: '[that which] moves everything [*alles Bewëgende*]' or 'The all-moving moves [*be-wëgt*] in that it speaks'.[113]

3.2   Let us now consider, word for word, a longer passage that most likely represents a well-encoded paraphrase of the concluding four lines of *Laozi* 25, and of the last line in particular. In von Strauss' translation they read: 'The measure [*Richtmass*] of the human is the earth, / the measure of the earth is heaven, / the measure of heaven is *dao*, / the measure of *dao* is itself'.[114] Wilhelm translates the last line as follows: 'Meaning [*der SINN*, *dao*] conforms [*richtet sich*] to itself'.[115] In the following paraphrase by Heidegger it helps to pay special attention to the word 'Appropriation' [*Ereignis*], which turns out to be an extremely important key-word, here presumably in a special sense with respect to *dao*, and more precisely for *dao fa zi ran* ['the measure of *dao* is itself'] in the Heideggerian paraphrase: 'Way, the appropriating-using way-making [*die er-eignend-brauchende Be-wëgung*]'.[116] Paraphrasing the aforementioned lines from the *Laozi*, Heidegger emphasizes the word 'Appropriation':

> The productive propriation [*Eignen*] that arouses Saying as show in its showing may be called 'appropriating' [*Ereignen*]. This produces [*er-gibt*] the Open of the clearing, in which what is present persists and

[112] 'The Nature of Language', in *WL* 87/*US* 192; 93/200; compare also 107/214.

[113] 'The Nature of Language', in *WL* 95/*US* 201; compare 95/202, 99/206, 107/215.

[114] Von Strauss, *Lao-Tse*, 89 [1870, 126]. The commentary reads: 'Just as humans, earth, and heaven have in each case their determining ground in something else, in something higher, so *dao* is determined by itself, "so of itself", as an expression of its absolute freedom' [259; 1870, 132]. Compare Buber, *Tschuang-Tse* 105, note 6, where the von Strauss translation of the last lines is quoted. Buber begins an attempt at a summary with the words: '*Dao* is *in itself* the unrecognizable, the unknowable. "The true *dao* does not explain itself".' Compare the section on *dao* in 'The Nature of Language' (92/198). We must also, of course, take into consideration the weeks-long collaboration between Hsiao and Heidegger on the attempt to translate those chapters of the *Laozi* that are concerned with a comprehensive understanding of *dao*.

[115] Wilhelm, *Laotse*, 65 [the translation of 1911 reads: 'And Meaning [*der Sinn*] has itself as a model [*hat sich selber zum Vorbild*]' (27)].

[116] 'The Way to Language', in *WS* 130/*US* 261. The complete sentence runs as follows: 'The Way to language as we first intended it does not become invalid, but rather becomes possible and necessary only through the *authentic* [*eigentlich*] Way, the appropriating-using way-making' (italics added). What more need be said to make this clearer? Perhaps, for the sake of comparison, the paraphrase with respect to *dao* in the sense of 'Saying': 'Being silent corresponds to the soundless chiming of the stillness of appropriating-showing Saying' (131/262). What an astonishing (and successful) turn of phrase from a *poetically* re-pondering *thinker* [des *nachdichtenden* Denkers]!

from which what is absent withdraws and can maintain its persistence in withdrawal. What appropriating produces through Saying [Way/*dao*] is never the effect of a cause, nor the consequence of a ground. Productive propriation, appropriating, is more granting than any effecting, making, and grounding. The appropriating is Appropriation [*das Ereignis*] itself – and nothing besides. Appropriation, seen in the showing of Saying [*dao*], can be understood neither as an occurrence nor as a happening but only experienced in the showing of Saying as that which grants. There is nothing else to which Appropriation leads back, from which it could be explained. Appropriating is not a product (result) of something else, but *the* Product [*die* (*sic.*) *Ergebnis*], from whose generous giving something like an 'It gives' can grant, and which even 'Being' needs in order to come into its own as presencing.

Appropriation gathers the design of Saying [*dao*] and develops it into the structure [*Gefüge*] of manifold showing. Appropriation is the most inconspicuous of the inconspicuous, the simplest of the simple, the nearest of the near, and the farthest of the far, in which we mortals spend our whole lives.

What holds sway in Saying [*dao*], Appropriation, can be named only by saying: It – Appropriation [*Ereignis*] – propriates [*eignet*].[117]

Drawing on the doctrine of *dao*, especially as exemplified in the relevant chapters of the *Laozi*, Appropriation is naturally for Heidegger 'not a law in the sense of a norm that hovers somewhere above us'.[118] The passage just quoted speaks clearly enough in its detailed paraphrasing the language of the *Dao de jing*, and especially of the last line of Chapter 25.[119]

There turns out to be a series of unmistakable resonances with doctrines of *dao* in the course of the two essays on language, the documentation and interpretation of which will be reserved for a later, more detailed exegesis. In what is for us by now a typical paraphrase (to give another example), Heidegger employs this formulation oriented specially towards *Laozi* 25: 'Language as world-moving [*Welt-bewëgende*] Saying [*dao*] is the relation [*Verhältnis*] of all relations'.[120] And also: 'Appropriation, propriating-holding-self-retaining, is the relation of all relations'.[121] With

---

[117] 'The Way to Language', in *WL* 127–8/*US* 258–9.

[118] 'The Way to Language', in *WL* 128/*US* 259. In this context Heidegger's reference to an obvious misunderstanding of the word 'law' for the Chinese *fa* seems suitable in so far as *fa* is sometimes rendered by 'law' [*Gesetz*] in the German translations of *Laozi* 25, even though 'take as a measure' (von Strauss), 'conform to' (Wilhelm), or even 'follow (the example of)' are more appropriate in this case. One can thus translate in this context: '*Dao* follows its own example', or '*Dao* follows itself of its own accord'.

[119] This passage may also reflect the results of Heidegger's subtle and nuanced attempts at translation (under the guidance of Hsiao and his competent interpretations of the text). See Hsiao, in *EMH* 126f.

[120] 'The Nature of Language', in *WL* 107/*US* 215.

[121] 'The Way to Language', in *WL* 135/*US* 267.

this the circle is closed. Appropriation is It itself, so of itself (*ziran*), 'and nothing besides',[122] just as *dao* is *dao*.[123]

In view of the topics that have been sketched here, it will now be easier to understand Heidegger's at first surprising claim to the effect that 'the *nature* [Wesen] of language can be nothing language-like' ('Conversation', 24/114), which is quite comprehensible in the light of Daoist ideas and resembles the Heideggerian dicta to the effect that the *Being* of beings can be nothing existent and the *nature* [Wesen] of the thing nothing thingly (see above, **3.2.1**).

3.3   The supposition that Heidegger has drawn from Daoist sources here again can be confirmed by a further remark in which he interprets his own thought. In the Le Thor seminar of 1969 he says unambiguously and in consonance with what has just been presented: 'With Appropriation one is no longer thinking in a Greek way at all' ('SLT' 104). He is thus apparently resuming his interpretation of Being (see Chapter 3), and he remarks, moreover, unambiguously that Being is appropriated by Appropriation ('SLT' 103).

Nor do these late remarks of Heidegger's stand alone.[124] For with respect to the *being* of language he says as early as 1951, a few years after his collaboration with Hsiao, 'Language would be Saying', following this with the statement: 'Even [the Greeks] themselves never *thought* this being [*Wesen*] of language, not even Heraclitus'.[125] But if Heidegger with

---

[122] It is interesting to note that Nietzsche concludes fragment 1067 of *The Will to Power* with the same phrase, 'and nothing besides' [*und nichts ausserdem*]. Heidegger (apparently following Nietzsche's example) employs this phrase as an emphatic formula not only here (*WL* 127/*US* 258) but also in the 'Letter on Humanism' – with respect to 'Being' (*BW* 236/*Wm* 188), as well as in the essay 'Language' – with respect to 'language' (*PLT* 190/*US* 12).

[123] In view of the recent publication of *Beiträge zur Philosophie* (1989, *GA* 65), which bears the heading 'Of Appropriation' ['Vom Ereignis'], it is advisable for our present purposes to postpone for the time being a detailed interpretation of the key Heideggerian term 'Appropriation'.

[124] Compare 'Logos', in *EGT* 78/*VA* 3:25.

[125] 'Logos', in *EGT* 77/*VA* 3:24. Compare 'Conversation', *WL* 39f/*US* 134f; 'Briefwechsel mit einem japanischen Kollegen', 6 [*JH*, 224]. It might be remarked further, by the way, that Heidegger employs the locution 'Language is the house of Being', which he first uses in the 'Letter on Humanism' (*BW* 193/*Wm* 145), on several occasions. In his pseudo-dialogue he remarks: 'Some time ago I called language, rather awkwardly, the house of Being' (*WL* 5/*US* 90 [also 21–2/111–12, 24/115, 26/117]). This locution is striking in its similarity to a formulation of Wilhelm von Humboldt's, who writes: 'Language ... is the organ of inner Being [*Seyn*], this Being itself' (*On Language*, 21/383 [7:14]). It is well known that Heidegger often employed von Humboldt's insights into language in his own thinking, frequently giving verbatim citations (see 'The Way to Language', in *WL* 136/*US* 268 [one page after another mentions language as 'the house of Being']; 'SLT' 87f). Compare **2.4**, footnote 48, above, and **3.1.1**, footnote 62. The question arises: Why not in this context, too? And possibly, why not also in many other contexts? Did Heidegger now and then put another meaning 'into the same housing [*Gehäuse*]' (von Humboldt)? Did he thereby merely confirm what Wilhelm von Humboldt had ascertained on the basis of his vast knowledge of languages and their interrelations? This and other such questions demand attention in this context. We are

his idea of Appropriation is no longer thinking in a Greek way at all, and not only here in the case of Appropriation, is he then thinking in a purely Heideggerian way – or in a somewhat Chinese way?

3.4 In view of his engagement with a number of non-Western *topoi* (or key-words), it is not improbable that Heidegger, with his penchant for poetic expression, received early on, long before *Being and Time*, inspiring and significant [weg*weisend*] stimulation from reading the appealing and delightful *Zhuangzi* of Martin Buber (1910), along with other works, and from being aided by knowledgeable conversation partners. Such stimulation might well have encouraged him, for example, to turn a phrase such as this: 'Being silent corresponds to the soundless chiming of the stillness of appropriating-showing Saying'.[126] In other words, being silent corresponds to *dao*.

This locution and other *topoi* that will simply be listed here – such as 'releasement', 'simplicity', 'renunciation', 'hiddenness', the 'fourfold', and 'nameless' (see **2.5**), as well as 'boundless', 'useless', and also 'enframing' [*Gestell*] in the context of the critique of technology[127] – can be traced more or less directly to the Martin Buber edition of the *Zhuangzi* (including Buber's 'Afterword'). They would thus not have escaped the notice of Martin Heidegger on his path [Way] of thinking.

grateful to Tilman Borsche for the following observation: 'Without engaging Humboldt closely, Heidegger, obviously feeling that a particular word is appropriate here, proposes to him and to the entire philosophical tradition the "task of *freeing* grammar from logic". . . . It . . . can hardly be denied that Humboldt himself recognized this task and – indeed within his own philosophical horizon – fulfilled it' (*Sprachansichten* [Stuttgart 1981], 232, note 21). Compare also Cho, *Bewusstsein und Natursein*, 260. The topic of von Humboldt and Heidegger naturally calls for thorough research on a variety of fronts.

[126] 'The Way to Language', in *WL* 131/*US* 262. Compare 135/266, 122/252; 'The Nature of Language', 108/215; 'Conversation', 52–3/152.

[127] See the anecdote concerning the well-sweep in 'The Gardener' (Buber, *Tschuang-Tse* 48/48–50).

5 A kind of confession

It is certainly good that the world knows only the beautiful work, and not also
its sources, nor the conditions of its origination; for knowledge of the springs
from which inspiration flowed to the artist would often confuse and shock
people, thereby annulling the effects of what is excellent.

Thomas Mann, *Death in Venice* (1912)

1 Our experiences with Heidegger's texts so far suggest that we might
try examining one of them to see whether it might not contain well-
encoded signs of a *confession*. In so far as it is a matter of rendering the
hidden meaning of a Heidegger text visible, one must also bear in mind
that Heidegger employs self-interpretations that cover up as well as clarify
or reinterpret, by virtue of which the true meaning is (in part) only
cautiously alluded to or else totally hidden or unsaid.[128] It is thus advisable to turn our attention to Heidegger's pseudo-dialogue (the
'Conversation' discussed in Chapter 2), a text in which an East Asian is
given 'the role' of a conversation partner in a very telling way; and it is
also advisable, in view of what has already been presented (in Chapters
2–4), to pay specially close attention to those passages that 'impart'
Heidegger's 'message' to us, even if 'hardly perceptibly' – thus ultimately
unmistakably.

Heidegger himself speaks of a 'confession', after saying, in the person
of his 'Japanese', 'As far as I am able to follow what you are saying, I
sense a *deeply hidden* kinship with our thinking, precisely because your

---

[128] Heidegger's masterfully oracular and esoteric remarks are – if one understands the striving
for greater depth of thought – extremely disturbing and off-putting, and they naturally make
our investigation more difficult precisely in as much as they readily encourage counter-
arguments (perhaps even calculated by Heidegger in advance). On the one hand, for
example, Heidegger writes (autobiographically): 'Subsequently [after the exciting years
between 1910 and 1914] what went well and failed to go well on the path that had been
chosen evades self-portrayal, which would only be able to name *what does not belong to
one*. And this is so for everything essential' (*Frühe Schriften* [Frankfurt a.M. 1972], foreword, xi [*GA* 1:57]; emphasis added). On the other hand, he says: 'It is a matter of a few
[!] people outside the public world working tirelessly to sustain a thinking that is attentive
to Being, knowing that this work has to aim at establishing a possibility of handing it down
to a distant future' ('SLT' 90).

path of thinking and its language are so totally other'.[129] Whereupon
Heidegger, in the role of the Inquirer in the fictitious dialogue, continues
pointedly with the words: 'Your confession arouses me in a way that I
can master only by our continuing our conversation'. Everything that
precedes and follows this (and especially the two adjacent pages of text)
constitutes in selected passages *Heidegger's* confession.

Heidegger admits, then, that there is a 'deeply hidden kinship' between
East Asian thought and his own attempts at thinking. But he is not further
prepared, aside from the occasional hint, to explicate the content or extent
of this kinship. Reticence is called for (*WL* 50/*US* 148), understandably,
for it is a matter (in accordance with *Laozi* 41) of leaving the Way
(*dao*) hidden and nameless. Consequently, Heidegger leaves his path of
thinking in the nameless (29/121; cf. 42/138) and yields neither to 'wanting
to know' (*Wissenwollen*) nor to the 'craving for explanations' (13/100).
For, according to the *Zhuangzi*, 'The nature of perfect *dao* is deeply
hidden [*tief verborgen*]; its reaches [*Weite*] lose themselves in the dark',
and 'the mania for knowing [*Wissenwahn*] is pernicious'.[130u] And with his
'Japanese' interlocutor he is of the opinion that it is not disturbing when
a conversation leaves what is really meant in indefiniteness, or even shelters it back into the indefinable (13/100). Heidegger's remaining silent is
to be understood as being in accord with and in the spirit of the doctrines
of *dao*, whatever Heidegger understands by being silent; and this silence
will at least be a part of his 'message', especially on his *nameless* path of
thinking, in accordance with the ancient teaching to the effect that one
who knows does not say (*Laozi* 56; cf. 73, 81). Moreover, 'simply to be
silent about silence' would have to be for Heidegger 'authentic saying
... and [would] remain the constant prelude to authentic conversation
on [von] language' (53/152).

But Heidegger remains silent only where it is opportune for him and
his secret; otherwise he is by no means silent [*schweigt*], but rather indulges
[*schwelgt*] in talk about the word 'silence', which here fits well – as it often
does – into his dramaturgy. Allusions are important for him, rather than
direct, easily understood answers to the questions he sets himself. His
concern is to 'present' in dialogue form indirect, encoded, and barely

---

[129] 'Conversation', in *WL* 40–1/*US* 136 (emphasis added).
[130] Buber, *Tschuang-Tse*, 42/43 – with which Heidegger was quite familiar. This is, of course,
by no means an isolated case of Heidegger's very skilful drawing on the (Buber edition of
the) *Zhuangzi* for locutions with which to characterize his own path of thinking. Moreover,
he even makes a veiled reference (indirect, perhaps, for good reason, and characteristically)
to Buber's *I and Thou* (Leipzig 1923) when he writes allusively: 'Even the much discussed
I-Thou experience belongs to the metaphysical realm of subjectivity' (*WL* 36/*US* 130). Under
these circumstances we shall leave aside the question whether Heidegger's distinguishing of
his own thinking from Buber's is at all valid. In this context an interesting remark made by
Fischer-Barnicol speaks for itself: 'When I mentioned Buber to him [Heidegger], he hardly
reacted, as if he knew this person only by name. I cannot imagine ... that he had read
anything by him' (*EMH* 93).

perceptible answers. In the 'Letter on Humanism' he even asks whether we should not simply endure the unavoidable misinterpretations of his work for a while longer (*BW* 225/*Wm* 176). What prompts his reticence is said to be growing insight into that which cannot be touched, which is veiled by the mystery of Saying (*dao*) (*WL* 50/*US* 148). In other words, Heidegger offers as something to be thought 'the gate of profound darkness, where the source of the primal inhibiting power lies'.[131] And here *remaining silent* is the dictate of the hour.

2 Heidegger's 'attempt at thinking' [*Denkversuch*] (19/109) apparently begins as early as 1920 with the lecture 'Phenomenology of Intuition and Expression' (*GA* 12:86)[v] – with a very early lecture then, to which Heidegger ascribes in his pseudo-dialogue not only an incorrect title but also a dubious transcript in Japan (the existence of the latter being in fact rather unlikely, since there could hardly have been any Japanese attending his lectures as early as the summer semester of 1920).[w] The entire lecture, according to Heidegger, remained allusive; he had simply continued to follow a faint 'trail' [*Wegspur*] – a *dao*-trail, surely (41/137).

In the absence of further clear indications, it is unusually difficult to reconstruct Heidegger's encoded *dao*-oriented attempts at thinking. He recommends 'attention to the trails that direct thinking into the region of its sources' (37/131); he finds such trails, he emphasizes, only because they do *not* come from him and are seldom perceptible (and now Heidegger waxes poetic), 'like a wind-borne echo of a distant call'.

A few sentences before this telling remark, Heidegger has his fictional interlocutor say something just as telling, to the effect that he [Heidegger] had asked his Japanese colleague Tanabe Hajime why the Japanese did not themselves reflect on the 'venerable beginnings' of their own thinking – which means in this context the ancient Daoist teachings, which form part of the source of Zen Buddhism. Heidegger thus proves to be with respect to East Asia someone acquainted with important relationships in the history of ideas.

In each case it is said to have been important for him to make visible 'the totally other' (34–5/128); the *fullness of Nothing*,[132] that which he had always, his whole life long, been saying (P 180/190). And in another context (again during the 1950s – such a productive period for him after

[131] Buber, *Tschuang-Tse*, 43/44. [There is also an allusion to the final line of the first chapter of the *Laozi*, reproduced on the front cover of *Ex oriente lux*, which speaks of profound darkness as 'the gate of all mysteries'.]
[132] See the little book bearing this title by Hōseki Shin'ichi Hisamatsu, *Die Fülle des Nichts: Vom Wesen des Zen. Eine systematische Erläuterung*, translated by Takashi Hirata and Johanna Fischer (Pfullingen 1980). Hisamatsu (1889–1980), one of the leading philosophers of religion in Japan, attempts from an East Asian and transcultural perspective to elucidate the peculiar nature of the Zen Buddhist understanding of nothingness. For comparative philosophy this is a valuable contribution which we must be content merely to mention at this point.

48   *Heidegger's hidden sources*

the attempts to translate the *Laozi* with his Chinese colleague Hsiao), coming back to the 'beginning' of a tradition of thinking, Heidegger writes, in a longer passage in 'Hölderlin's Earth and Sky' that serves as a clear amplification of what has just been presented:

> What is changing [in Europe] is able to do so only thanks to the *preserved* greatness of its beginning. Accordingly the present state of the world can receive an *essential* [*wesenhaft*] transformation – or even just the preparation for it – only from its own beginning, which determines our era through destiny [*geschicklich*]. It is the great beginning. There is *of course no going back* to it. The present as something waiting over against us becomes the great beginning only in its coming towards the small [*zum Geringen*]. But nor can this small something remain any longer in its *Western* isolation. It is opening up to the few *other* great beginnings that belong with their Own to *the Same* of the beginning of the infinite relationship, within which the earth is held.[133]

3   In China, then, or in the larger sphere of East Asian culture as one of the few other great beginnings, Heidegger finds what is *for him* 'the totally other', which, he writes, gradually transformed his thinking in the way that going on a hike involves leaving one place in favour of another (42/138); for no one can simply leap out of the prevailing realm of ideas, especially when it is a matter of paths of thinking that have been travelled for so long (36/130). Thus Heidegger left one place, the place of metaphysics, in favour of another, which he characteristically leaves, encoded, 'without name' (42/138 – *for* dao *is hidden and without name* [*Laozi* 41]).

In a later passage and in a somewhat different context, which may finally bring us closer to the solution of the enigma, Heidegger is again eloquently reticent in saying: 'If I . . . could answer that now, the darkness enveloping the Way would be dissipated [*gelichtet*]' (49/147–8). The secret of *dao* would then be given away and the consequences would be immeasurable. 'But perhaps', Heidegger writes on another occasion, where he could hardly be more clear unless he were to give away his secret after all,

> the answer to these questions [from where (briefly) the thinking of Being receives its direction] will some day come from just those attempts at thinking that distinguish themselves, as do mine, as anarchic arbitrariness [quite in the spirit of *Laozi* 18, 19, 38, 57]. . . . Everything here is Way [cf. *WL* 92/*US* 198] of a *corresponding* that examines as it listens. Way is always in danger [*Weg*, used here without the article, probably stands for *dao*] of becoming error [*Irrweg* – or

---

[133] 'Hölderlins Erde und Himmel', in *Hölderlin-Jahrbuch* 11 (1958–60):36 (emphases added). [Also in Heidegger's *Erläuterungen zu Hölderlins Dichtung* (fourth, expanded edition, Frankfurt a.M. 1971), 177.]

Holzweg, woodpath]. To go such ways demands practice in going. Practice requires craft [*Handwerk*].[134]

Bearing in mind the *totally other*, Heidegger now presents himself in the spirit of the *Zhuangzi* as the 'border-crosser of the borderless',[135x] who is at the same time 'message-bearer of the message'.[136] The 'border-crosser of the borderless' – that is, of 'Nothing', 'emptiness', 'clearing', of the 'Open'[137] – thinks only this *single* thought: 'Being: Nothing: Same'.[138] For, according to Heidegger, the thinker needs only a single thought, to think this One as *the Same* and to speak of this Same in the appropriate way; thus for thinking, the borderless [*das Grenzenlose*] of the Same is the sharpest border.[139]

Under the circumstances, one would expect in this 'confession' something on the topic of 'Saying'. Correspondingly, Heidegger drops the encoded hint that it is only with insight into the 'nature [*Wesen*] of Saying' (*dao*) that thinking first starts out on the Way that takes us back from merely metaphysical representation towards attention to the hints of that 'message' whose special 'bearer' he (with his fictitious interlocutor) would like to become (47–8/145–6). This Way is, however, long, as he would have us bear in mind. Nevertheless (we can amplify by means of another passage), thinking-poetizing would have to go back to where it had always already been in a certain sense, but had not yet built [*baute*]; thinking-poetizing would, however, have to content itself with making [*bauen*] the 'Way' that would lead back to the site where metaphysics is overcome.[140] In this manner, one must add, thinking would devote itself to a wondrous way-building [*Wegebau*], in which the builders would sometimes have to go back to abandoned building-sites or even back beyond them (21/110).

This is how Heidegger's departure from the place of metaphysics comes about, as finally expressed unequivocally in the telling phrase 'departure from all *It is*' (54/154). In the meantime Heidegger, in his attempting consonance with the teachings of Daoism and Zen Buddhism, often employs 'simple Saying', and in such a way that 'language speaks'

---

[134] 'Afterword [to the lecture 'The Thing']: A Letter to a Young Student' (1950), in *PLT* 185–6 / *VA* 2:58–9.
[135] [*Grenzgänger des Grenzenlosen*] 'Conversation', in *WL* 41/*US* 137. See Buber, *Tschuang-Tse* 76/76 (Chapter 22); in the Stange edition, p. 69.
[136] [*Botengänger der Botschaft*] 'Conversation', in *WL* 40, 41, 48/*US* 136, 137, 146, etc.
[137] 'Conversation', in *WL* 19, 20, 41, 46/*US* 108, 110, 137, 144.
[138] 'SLT' 101. See the discussion in **3.1.1** above.
[139] *WCT?*, 50/20. Compare 'From the Experience of Thinking', in *PLT* 4/'Aus der Erfahrung des Denkens', *GA* 13:76; 'Vorbemerkung', in *Wm*, *GA* 9:ix. [In the 'Vorbemerkung' Heidegger characterizes that which determines the matter of thinking as demanding that one reside 'in the constantly sought sameness of the Same'.]
[140] *QB* 103–5/*Wm* 251. Compare the 'Conversation', where the transformation [*Verwandlung*] of thinking would take place as a hike [*Wanderung*] on which one place [*Ort*] would be left in favour of another, which would then require *explanation* [Erörterung]; one place would be metaphysics, while the other will be left [by Heidegger and his interlocutor] without name (*WL* 42/*US* 138).

[*die Sprache spricht*] as the 'thing things' [*das Ding dingt*].[141] Consequently, one must turn one's attention to a 'totally other' direction. This look, according to Heidegger, is *in its way* Greek and yet with respect to what is seen no longer Greek nor *ever* can be (39/135). As for what it is, however, there is thus for Heidegger even at this point no direct answer. An answer seems superfluous, since there now follows what is for the careful reader his dramatized 'confession' of the 'deeply hidden kinship' (41/136). And with this we find ourselves back at the starting-point of our decoding of this remarkable pseudo-dialogue that has so far received so little attention. If at all, one comes to expect no more than this kind of confession from Heidegger.

---

[141] See above, **3.2.1**. Compare 'Language', in *PLT* 190f, 197f, 199–200/*US* 12f, 19f, 22. This text could provide further material, in so far as Heidegger, as he remarks later, '[had] ventured something provisional' ('Conversation', 49/147); this would probably be true only of the *lecture*, for 'the printed version represents in part a substantial elaboration of the second version [of the lecture]' (*US*, in *GA* 12:259), which is for us less rich. Compare also 'The Turning', in *QT* 43, 49 ['Die Kehre', 42, 46].

6 Conclusions

1.1 The foregoing investigation has shown that Heidegger's work was influenced by East Asian sources to a hitherto unrecognized extent. Moreover, it seems highly probable that Heidegger, without stating his sources, in a number of cases of central importance appropriated ideas germane to his work from German translations primarily of Daoist classics but presumably of Zen Buddhist texts as well.

Case 1

As the juxtaposition of relevant textual passages has shown (see **3.2.1**), Heidegger adopts almost verbatim, in order to articulate the *topos* 'Nothing' in a non-Western way, locutions from Chapter 22 of the *Zhuangzi* in the translation by Richard Wilhelm – to the effect that the thingness of the thing cannot itself be a thing.

Case 2

The earlier formulation 'The Being of beings 'is' not itself a being' (*SZ* 6) apparently anticipates the 'thing'-locution in terms of sentence structure and meaning. Drawing on Victor von Strauss' commentary on Chapter 2 of the *Laozi* – and the corresponding locution in the *Shinjinmei* in Ōhazama – Heidegger then writes in further clarification of his 'new' thinking: 'Being and Nothing are not given beside one another. Each uses itself on behalf of the other'. And: 'Nothing and Being the Same' (see the juxtapositions in **3.1.3**).

Case 3

With respect to the *topos* 'Nothing', Heidegger obviously formulates the synonymous *topos* 'Emptiness', drawing this time on Chapter 11 of the *Laozi* in Wilhelm's translation, which has the thingly nature of the container consisting in *emptiness* (see the discussion in **3.2.2**).

Cases 4 and 5

In his pseudo-dialogue 'From a Conversation on Language', Heidegger adopts almost verbatim, but well hidden, two formulations from a text by Oscar Benl on Noh drama (see **2.4**). While these two instances do not affect Heidegger's major ideas of East Asian provenance, they nevertheless provide further evidence of the manner in which he integrates foreign ways of thinking into his own texts without indicating their source.

Case 6

Drawing on the idea of *dao* in the sense of both Way and Saying, as expressed by Richard Wilhelm and Martin Buber, Heidegger clearly formulates his correspondence between Way and Saying (see **4.2**).

Further cases beyond these can probably be adduced (see, especially, **4.3.4**). Another case of striking correspondence suggests that Heidegger conceived his key idea of 'Appropriation' on the model of the concluding trope of Chapter 25 of the *Laozi* (see **4.3.2–3**).

Taken together, these cases show that Heidegger very probably thought through and deliberately elaborated his path-breaking ideas from as early as the 1920s on, drawing particularly from the above-mentioned texts of Victor von Strauss, Richard Wilhelm, and mainly from Martin Buber's *Tschuang-Tse*, without ever giving the customary indications of the sources of his thinking. His subsequent appropriation of East Asian ways of thinking, effected through encoded presentations, was presumably furthered in no small measure by his conversations with Chinese and Japanese scholars, though obviously unbeknown to those interlocutors (see Chapters 1, 2, and 7). As became known only after his death, Heidegger's collaboration with Paul Hsiao in the summer of 1946 played an important role in this respect (see **1.2.2**). This is also confirmed in the connection with Hsiao's account by the letter of 9 October 1947 in which Heidegger expresses the desire to continue his conversations with him again soon (see **1.1**).

1.2 The assumption that these correspondences are merely fortuitous can be rejected on the basis of their nature and quantity (Chapters 2–4); they become especially numerous in the texts from the 1950s, following the period during which Heidegger collaborated with Hsiao on translating the *Laozi*. The nature and quantity of the correspondences suggest a deliberate appropriation of East Asian ways of thinking. It is highly improbable that Heidegger, whose interest in East Asian thought is uncontested, who was able to appreciate it, and even admitted being familiar with most of the relevant texts we have mentioned, should have happened to think and write in such a closely parallel manner in the passages adduced above merely by chance. And the same is of course true for numerous other passages in which Heidegger, as we have seen, thinks in a similarly East Asian way.

The assumption of mere coincidence needs to be rejected also on the basis of Heidegger's 'confession' (see Chapter 5, above). In an encoded manner, yet unambiguously, he speaks of a 'deeply hidden kinship' between his own and East Asian thinking. In other words, he speaks of a connection based on his adoption of some essential traits of East Asian thinking which, for reasons easy to understand, he declined to reveal.

In contrast, the passage from the '*Der Spiegel* conversation' (see **1.2.3**) must be understood as a tactically necessary 'cover-up' manoeuvre that turned out to be necessary for the preservation of his secret (see **5.4**).[142] Heidegger's letter to his Japanese colleague Kojima Takehiko, written on 18 August 1963 and published a year before the *Der Spiegel* conversation (**3.2.2**), also speaks in favour of this interpretation. There Heidegger indicates quite decisively, if again in an encoded manner, what has determined his path of thinking: 'above all not a reanimation of the beginning of Western philosophy'[143] – even though one is happy to assume the contrary in the West.

2.1 In so far as Heidegger's work has been influenced by East Asian sources, it is not simply a matter of peripheral topics that are thought about merely incidentally. In the case of the *topos* 'Nothing' (**3.1** and **3.2**) it is a matter – bearing in mind the locution 'Nothing and Being the Same' – of *the* major idea, the 'only one' the thinker needs (*WCT* 50/20); a matter, then, of an idea that is new to Western thinking, and which Heidegger owes to insight into the teachings of *dao* in the *Laozi* and *Zhuangzi*. For Heidegger, 'Nothing' is not merely a nugatory nothing, the nothingness of nihilism: it is rather the 'Nothing of Being [*Seyn*]', *fullness* (see **1.1**). He pursues this thought in his texts continually, which are in this context striking for their repetitions and variations of 'the Same'.[144] To effect a complete and conclusive clarification he eventually (in 1969) adds the 'simple' formula: 'Being: Nothing: Same' ('SLT' 101). Corresponding Daoist- and Zen Buddhist-tinged paraphrases are to be found (see Chapters 3 and 4), in more or less encoded form, throughout the work that has been published so far.

Whereas in the formula 'Being: Nothing: Same' the 'Same' constitutes a conspicuous key word (*WCT* 50/20) for a better understanding of Heidegger's work in general, one that holds together in a hidden way all the identifications discussed above, thought of as corresponding *silently*

---

[142] Compare the different interpretation of this passage in Cho, *Bewusstsein und Natursein*, 16 [who takes Heidegger's assertion of the irrelevance of Zen Buddhism at face value].

[143] 'Briefwechsel mit einem japanischen Kollegen', 6 [*JH*, 224].

[144] On Heidegger's view it is precisely this thought that has been misunderstood in the West (see **3.1.1** above, especially the passage [*WL* 19/*US* 108–9] cited in note 69).

with the spirit of the Daoist teachings, the reader must first laboriously explicate the identification of Way and Saying in order to see that here, too, Heidegger's thinking draws significantly from East Asian sources (see Chapter 4, above).

2.2.1 The preceding investigation has not only shown *what* Heidegger has appropriated but also *how* he has paraphrased the adopted ways of thinking and integrated them into his texts in such a way that hardly a trace remains of their East Asian sources. We were able to point at the beginning of the investigation to a valuable document that now assumes considerable weight. For it shows quite explicitly how Heidegger paraphrases a German translation of a passage from *Laozi* 15 in such a way that his text eventually becomes so distant from the wording of the translation that the major *topoi* of the Daoist teachings find expression in his adaptation (and diction) as corresponding key terms in his own thinking.

The document is Heidegger's letter to Hsiao of 9 October 1947, which came to light only after forty years through being printed in the volume *Heidegger and Asian Thought*. In this brief letter Heidegger takes Hsiao's translation of a passage from the *Laozi*, which Hsiao had carefully explained to him character by character during their collaboration the previous year, as the basis for two versions of his own (see **1.1** above). While the first appears to stem from the earlier collaborative translation work, and renders understandable Hsiao's discomfort with such 'transposition' (see *EMH* 126),ʸ the second has hardly anything to do with Hsiao's translation, which at best stays in the background 'like the wind-borne echo of a distant call' ('Conversation', 37/131). A comparison of the texts easily reveals to the practised interpreter how Heidegger is proceeding here and what his aim is. (The discussion that follows concerns the passages quoted on pp. 2f above).

The addition of the phrase 'the *dao* of heaven' may be acceptable in the context of a broadly conceived interpretation,[145] but this is not the case with the question preceding it ['Who is able by making tranquil (*stil-lend*) to bring something in to Being?']. For here Heidegger would appear to go far beyond the original text in alluding with the word *stillend* (*not* moving, in the sense of the resting of any kind of movement) – posited as synonymous with 'Nothing' in the sense of 'Nothing and Being the Same' (see **3.1.3**) – to 'Being'.[146ᶻ] The result is that Nothing brings, through nothinging [*nichtend*], beings ('something') 'into Being' – something that

---

[145] This is how Hsiao seems to have understood Heidegger's supplement in connection with his original calligraphy of the verse for Heidegger (see *HAT* 100).
[146] Compare the 'Afterword to "What Is Metaphysics?" ': ' "Being" (*Austrag*) as the soundless voice, the voice of stillness [*Stimme der Stille*]' (*GA* 9:306, footnote f). [The note is appended to the word 'soundless' in the context of the possibility of experiencing Being through not shrinking in the face of 'the soundless voice that summons to the terror of the abyss' (*Wm* 102).]

in Daoism only *dao* could do (see **3.1.2**). This, then, explains the answer Heidegger appended (referring to Hsiao's calligraphy) to the question. His first version could now serve well as a basis for the second. This second version represents a creative and eloquent 'recomposition' influenced by the relationships (discussed above) among *wu* (Nothing), *yu* (Being), and *dao* (Way/Saying), in Heideggerian terminology, such that we have before us the key words that Heidegger drew from Daoist teachings as early as the 1920s and 1930s, and which eventually, after the collaborative translation with Hsiao of the chapters in the *Laozi* dealing with *dao*, extensively condition his subsequent thinking – above all during the 1950s.[147a]

One can see in the way Heidegger writes the verb 'move' [*be-wegen*] (playing on *dao*, Way [*Weg*], even though the Chinese word for 'move' in the *Laozi* text does not provide any 'etymological' warrant for this) an indication of how the 'multi-layered meaning of the Chinese text' (Hsiao, *EMH* 127) can be made 'thinkable and clear in a Western language' (even in Heidegger's idiosyncratic diction and interpretation, which go beyond the original). Our previous investigation (in Chapter 4, above) attempted to clarify the way this 'moving' [*be-wegen*] flowed into Heidegger's texts on language (with the 'e'-trema in *wëgen* and other combinations).[148]

2.2.2 In this context Heidegger's often repeated associations of thinking [*Denken*] and poetizing [*Dichten*] gain a special meaning, in so far as the great teachers of classical Daoism are poets as well as thinkers, and Zhuangzi, to whom Heidegger owes so much, is the greatest among them. Heidegger may well have taken Zhuangzi as a significant model to measure himself by, and not only Hölderlin, Rilke, George, or Trakl – to name just a few Western figures who have played a similar role for him. Heidegger the poet, as opposed to Heidegger the thinker, would not then be expected to observe the custom of citing the sources underlying the 'beautiful' work, for knowledge of those, as Thomas Mann so aptly remarks, would 'often confuse and shock, thereby annulling the effects of what is excellent'. That would be fine – if only Heidegger did not lay claim to being understood and taken seriously as a thinker! But thinking and poetizing are so closely intertwined in him that one is hardly to be

---

[147] The role the *Laozi* chapter may have played in Heidegger's 'Discussion of *Gelassenheit*' ['Conversation on a Country Path about Thinking'], which was published in 1959 but supposedly written in 1944/5, is shown, for example, by a short passage (*DT* 70/*GA* 13:51) for which Heidegger drew, presumably before his collaboration with Hsiao, from the version of *Laozi* 15 by Wilhelm (*Laotse*, 134) and/or that by von Strauss (*Lao-Tse*, 74, 230f). The later versions in the letter to Hsiao would then be simply the expression of new (and deeper) endeavours at appropriation.

[148] See section 3 of both 'The Nature of Language' and 'The Way to Language'; the coinage *wëgen* occurs in the latter essay (*WL* 129f/*US* 261f).

distinguished from the other.[149] This is because *thinking*, as Heidegger proclaims, has to *poetize* in response to the enigma of Being.[150]

Is it, therefore, so astonishing that one has had to admit – with regard to a thinking that issues in enigmas and likes to create an abundance of encoded locutions (in other words, concealed plays on Daoist teachings which have gone unrecognized) – that, as Walter Biemel has said,[151] we have still not managed to achieve a proper dialogue with Heidegger, because the partner has not been there and we have been genuinely taken aback by this thinking?

2.3   This kind of thinking *and* poetizing under East Asian influence has again taken (post-Nietzsche) as its major task the overcoming of metaphysics, the basic trait of which Heidegger sees as 'onto-theo-logic' (*ID* 59/50). Where this thinking has from early on received its ('silent') directive from[152] is now not difficult to surmise.[153] *From ancient Chinese thought* – for metaphysics, so conceived, was never developed there.[154] Being neither indebted to Aristotelian logic[155b] nor receptive to an ontology involving a subject–object dichotomy, nor, above all, being conditioned by any theology, ancient Chinese thought was completely remote from the assertion of 'eternal truths', which belong according to Heidegger 'to the residue of Christian theology that has still not been properly eradicated from philosophical problematics' (*SZ* 229). On this issue, what could be closer to the mark than Heidegger's saying that his thinking (under East Asian influence, to be consistent) could be 'theistic' as little as 'atheistic'.[156]

Thus Heidegger, 'as message-bearer' of his message (see **5.3**), recommends under*way* that the lacunae left in the greatness of the Western

---

[149] See 'What Are Poets For?', in *PLT* 99–100/*Hw* 256; 'The Thinker as Poet', in *PLT* 12/*GA* 13:84. Compare also Karl Löwith, *Denker in dürftiger Zeit* (Göttingen 1953, 1965), 11 [where Löwith writes: 'It is for the most part undecidable whether Heidegger poetizes thinkingly or thinks poetically, so much does he poetically condense a thinking that is associatively disintegrated'].

[150] 'The Anaximander Fragment', in *EGT* 58/*Hw* 343; compare 'Logos', in *EGT* 78/*VA* 3:25.

[151] See Walter Biemel, 'Dichtung und Sprache bei Heidegger', in *Man and World* 2/4 (1969):487–514, 490; also his *Heidegger* (Hamburg 1973), 129.

[152] See 'A Letter to a Young Student', in *PLT* 185/*VA* 2:58 [where Heidegger remarks that he finds it 'strange' that people should ask 'from where [his] thinking receives its directive [*Weisung*]'].

[153] It was not from pre-Socratic thought, nor from Western (theo-)mystical thinking, nor from Nietzsche's poetic thinking, nor even from Hölderlin's poetry that Heidegger received the *essential* impetus for his 'new' poetic thinking. One can hardly help but think that the Western thinkers and poets he mentions simply serve to help him further, step by step, his significant [*wegweisend*] work through so-called dialogue with them, without his attempting or sustaining an *authentic* interpretation of them.

[154] See Hajime Nakamura, *Ways of Thinking of Eastern Peoples: India – China – Tibet – Japan* (Honolulu 1964,⁵ 1971), 243–6; Joseph Needham, *Science and Civilization in China*, vol. 2: History of Scientific Thought (Cambridge 1956, ⁴1975), 37.

[155] Hsiao instructed Heidegger on this point; see *EMH* 128.

[156] 'Letter on Humanism', in *BW* 230/*Wm* 182.

beginning (see 'Hölderlin's Earth and Heaven' 36) be gradually filled by the teaching of 'the fullness of Nothing'.[c] This, too, could ultimately communicate Heidegger's 'confession' to us (see **5.2**).

3 If one agrees with Walter Biemel's assertion that an interpretation must open the text up and be able to show what lies hidden in a thinker's thought and what it is grounded upon,[157] then the present investigation can also be seen as a small contribution to the interpretation of Heidegger. At any rate, the full extent of its consequences for appropriate future interpretations can at this point hardly be gauged.

In order to gain a new perspective from this 'Heidegger case', we in the West will have to devote ourselves to *non-Western* thinking as thoroughly as to that of our own tradition, not least since Heidegger has, in his own special way, demonstrated the necessity of *transcultural* thinking.

Thanks to Goethe's having rendered great service to the cause of world literature, such a field is now, a good hundred-and-fifty years later, firmly established; but 'world philosophy', by contrast, is still a long way off. Nevertheless, Karl Jaspers sees here 'the unavoidable task of the era'.[158] And to this task Martin Heidegger, too, has paid tribute in a unique way.

---

[157] Walter Biemel, *Heidegger*, 129.
[158] Hans Saner, *Jaspers* (Reinbek bei Hamburg 1970), 105 (cf. 103–10).

7 Tezuka Tomio, 'An Hour with Heidegger'[159]

Translation[d]

At the end of March 1954 I visited Professor Heidegger in Freiburg, where I was able to hear what he had to say about the significance of present-day Christianity for European culture. I first reported on this issue in a column for the *Tōkyō Shinbun* [newspaper] towards the end of January 1955. In my concern about the psychological and spiritual condition of the Japanese today, I find that this issue comes up again and again in my thinking; and for that reason I made it the topic of my questions to Professor Heidegger.[e] However, during the first part of our conversation Heidegger asked me various questions concerning the Japanese way of thinking and Japanese art, and had me talk about them. Since I am often asked about how the conversation went, I should like to write a few words about it here.

Heidegger's interest in Japan appears to have been first aroused by the late Kuki Shūzō, about whom he spoke very fondly. A man from Kyoto, Uchigaki Keiichi, had visited Heidegger in Freiburg some time before, and Heidegger had asked him for a photograph of Kuki's grave in Kyoto. Mr Uchigaki accordingly wrote home and had several photographs sent, which Heidegger now showed me. The natural stone of the headstone, the beautifully scripted epitaph, the surrounding plantings – the entire well-planned grave is one of the most elegant I have ever seen. In its synthesis of the natural and the artificial, it conveyed a comprehensive sense of the refinement of Japanese sensibility.

The conversation then continued naturally on topics connected with Japan. Heidegger mentioned D. T. Suzuki and said that he [Heidegger]

[159] The original Japanese text was published with Tezuka Tomio's translation of 'From a Conversation on Language' in *Haideggā zenshū* (*Heidegger: Complete Works*) (Tokyo: Risō, 1975), vol. 21, 3rd edition, 159–66. The author, Tezuka Tomio (1903–83), was Professor of German literature at Tokyo University and a member of the Japanese Academy. Among his major works are *Modern German Poets*, *In Search of the Spirit of Western Europe*, *Studies on [Stefan] George and Rilke*. He also translated such works as Heidegger's *Explanations of Hölderlin's Poetry* and 'What Are Poets For?'; *Goethe's Collected Poems*; Carossa, *The Year of Beautiful Deceptions*; Hesse, *Siddhartha*; Nietzsche, *Thus Spoke Zarathustra*. (Reinhard May thanks Professor Klaus Müller and Mr Shigenobu Maehara for looking through his translation.)

was interested in Zen thinking, which is open to a vast world. In general, scholars and thinkers in the West make frequent mention of Suzuki.

My reading of Heidegger's work has been mainly concerned with his discussions of poetry. It seems to me that, for Heidegger, what is most essential about human existence is concentrated in language, and that he therefore tries to understand human existence and its workings on the basis of instances where language comes forth purely and with forceful energy (as happens in the best poetry). And so what he wanted to hear from me was something *of* the Japanese language – not just something *about* Japanese language, but the language itself.

> Higher than the lark,
> ah, the mountain pass!
> – quietly resting.[f]

Heidegger had read this haiku by Bashō in German translation and had been very impressed by it, and so he asked me to write it down for him, in romanization as well as in Japanese characters, and to give a word-by-word explication. He read the romanized version to himself silently. He expressed his feeling about it by saying that one can sense a vast world in such a simple expression, and that what is simple is not without content.

He then asked me: 'In Japanese there is presumably a word for language so-called: what is the original meaning of this word?'

I replied: 'The word you are asking about is *kotoba*. Since I am not a specialist in this area, I cannot offer a precise account, but I think that the *koto* is connected with *koto* [meaning "matter"] of *kotogara* [meaning "event" or "affair" (*Sache*)]. The *ba* is a sound-transformation of *ha* and has connotations of "many" or "dense", as with leaves (*ha*) on a tree. If this is right, then the *koto* of "language" and the *koto* of "matter" are two sides of the same coin: things happen and become language (*kotoba*). The word "*kotoba*" may have its roots in ideas of this kind'.

This explanation seemed to fit well with Heidegger's ideas. Taking notes on a piece of paper that was to hand, he said: 'Very interesting! In that case, Herr Tezuka, the Japanese word for "language", *kotoba*, can mean *Ding* [thing]'.

There was perhaps an element here of forcing the word into a preconceived idea, but I was not in a position to contradict this interpretation. 'Perhaps one can say that', I replied. 'In my opinion it could mean thing [*Ding*] as well as affair [*Sache*]'.

'Isn't that so? Have you read my essay "The Thing"? I wrote something there that bears upon this issue. If you read it, please let me hear your impressions'.

The conversation then turned to the topic of the special nature of Japanese art. Even though this is not my own area of research, I nevertheless let Heidegger know what I had been feeling – especially since leaving Japan – about this issue. 'A distinctive feature of the Japanese people and, correspondingly, of Japanese art is its aesthetic sensibility. The Japanese are weak in speculative and abstract thinking and conceiving, and also not very motivated. One proceeds in all matters clearly and concretely on the basis of what is given by the senses and feelings. Japanese art distinguishes itself by not being content with a mere reproduction of sensory impressions, but is rather inclined, as the degree of artistic sensibility increases, to let what is grasped by the senses gradually assume a symbolic character. And so even when the minutest things are brought to expression, they are often connected in various ways with spatiality. In short, even insignificant things (*mono*) or matters (*koto*) can have the meaning of their being enhanced through being transposed into a vast space. I think one could say in this regard that there is a spiritual character to Japanese art that goes beyond its sensory characteristics. One strives for spirituality by way of the sensory. I think that this is what more or less distinguishes Japanese art. One admittedly finds from time to time a consciously opposite attitude, but in general this characteristic seems to be valid'.

In response to this Heidegger again introduced some of his favourite terms of art. 'Herr Tezuka, could one also say that this so-called spiritual character is metaphysical in nature?' After briefly pondering the question I assented, even though I felt that one would have to append an explanation of the Japanese understanding of metaphysics. Heidegger was clearly pleased, and went on to say: 'The Platonic Idea is also something metaphysical that is mediated through the senses; and yet there is a division into two levels. But in the case of Japan, I have the feeling that the two are more of a unity . . .'

Heidegger's interest in the Japanese language was manifested in connection with this problem as well. 'Which words in Japanese are the customary terms for appearance [*Erscheinung*] and essence [*Wesen*]? I don't want technical terms. Can't one express these ideas in words that are used in everyday speech?'

These were difficult questions. After searching through the appropriate vocabulary in my memory, I said the following: 'One can't regard these words as "everyday" exactly: they were originally Buddhist terms that were consciously employed in thinking. But I believe they have been familiar to the Japanese for long enough and are sufficiently widely used that they have achieved the status of everyday words. I am thinking of *shiki* and *kū*, where *shiki* would correspond to appearance and *kū*, generally speaking, to essence. Moreover, in Buddhist thought and in the thinking of the Japanese, which bears a close relationship to it, these two stand in contrast to one another and at the same time are conceived as one and the same. More so than in the case of philosophical thinking, this issue has been absorbed, one might say, into the experience of ordinary people in a smooth and natural manner. That is why these terms can be given in answer to your question. The conception of this one-and-the-same is the so-called *shiki soku kū* and *kū soku shiki* way of thinking, an idea that is rooted deep within our consciousness. To characterize the meanings of these words in more detail, *shiki* would be colour and colouring, and, by extension, appearance; and though *kū* originally means emptiness, or sky (*sora*), it also means 'the open' (the opened-up world). In one respect it is empty nothing (*kū mu*), although this doesn't have a merely negative meaning, but rather refers to the primordial way of being of all things, and thus to a condition that is striven for as an ideal. Buddhist doctrine is especially aware of this. As far as the symbolic character of Japanese art is concerned, it ultimately symbolizes this kind of emptiness (*kū*); and when such a thing takes place, it is regarded as magnificent in the extreme. Precisely there where appearance (*shiki*) is emptiness (*kū*), appearance begins to approach what is essential. This premonition of the essential is thus oriented to this empty nothing and limitlessness, which is the traditional orientation of our ways of thinking and feeling. You mentioned earlier, Herr Professor, the metaphysical character of Japanese art; but I believe that it is a metaphysical character of this kind. In my opinion, Japanese art is ultimately in some sense an art of space – which has its advantages as well as limitations'.

Heidegger showed great interest, and again took notes, throughout this response. He expressed a desire to read Japanese literature, in English translation if necessary. When he inquired about the literary basis of the film [by Kurosawa] *Rashōmon*, I told him that it came from a story by the modern Japanese author Akutagawa Ryūnosuke, and that one could also discern an influence from Browning in the original story. When I asked about his impressions of *Rashōmon*, the elderly Professor replied emphatically: 'It was very interesting'. I felt that the kind of indefiniteness conveyed by this film concerning our knowledge of reality may have intrigued Heidegger as an East Asian phenomenon. It is another question, of course, whether one can regard this work as a pure exemplification of this East Asian characteristic.

In short, during the first half of the conversation with Heidegger I had to do most of the talking in response to his series of rapidly posed questions, though I could sense the direction of his interest from the ways the questions were put. When I mentioned 'the open' as a possible translation of *kū* (emptiness) I already had a premonition that this would sit well with him as an interpreter of Hölderlin and Rilke. He was pleased indeed! 'East and West', he said, 'must engage in dialogue at this deep level. It is useless to do interviews that merely deal with one superficial phenomenon after another'. He then showed me several books containing his latest essays, and I was delighted to receive an offprint of his piece on [Georg] Trakl. He touched on the superficial phenomena of this world only when he asked my opinion of the future relations between communist China and the Soviet Union.

Heidegger seemed to notice that he had made me do most of the talking up to this point. 'From now on', he said, 'please ask whatever you like'.

In my role as a scholar of German literature, I asked him his views on the current state of research in Germany. He mentioned Emil Staiger in Zürich in particular, saying that he played a central role in literary theory. He appreciated Staiger's interpretive methodology, but added that it had found almost too many followers.

I was eager to hear something about Heidegger's essay 'What Are Poets For?' (in the book with the Japanese title *Poets in a Destitute Time*). In this essay, the title of which borrows from a line of Hölderlin's, when Heidegger writes that Rilke resembles Hölderlin in being a poet who takes on a task in a destitute time, he thereby elaborates his own thinking. But in my capacity as a scholar of German poetry, I was more interested in learning about Heidegger's view of Rilke than about his own thinking. That Hölderlin was truly a 'poet in a destitute time' is evident not only from the ideas in his poetry but more so from its purely mournful and painful tone. Since both Heidegger and I were lovers of Hölderlin there could be no difference of opinion on this matter. Nor was this any gratuitous judgement on our part: we could confirm it at any time simply by referring to the poems. But in my opinion, Rilke is extremely problematic on this point. In order to count as a 'poet in a destitute time', a poet would have to cultivate a deep-seated love for his time as well as for the people of that time, however cut off from it he might appear to be. Things may be different with Rilke, at the core. There is a danger of getting only a partial grasp of the ideas in his poems and taking him as a 'poet of love'. Now while Heidegger wanted precisely to take Rilke as a 'poet in a destitute time' in the style of Hölderlin and as a 'poet of love', he was reticent in his conclusion, and expressed himself unclearly, in writing '*if* Rilke is a poet in a destitute time'.[8] I asked him: 'Professor Heidegger, is there a special reason for your writing "if" there?' He got up and fetched the volume *Holzwege* in which this essay is reprinted. He opened the book to the passage in question and asked, 'You mean this passage?' He then answered my question by saying, 'That's right. I avoided a clear judgement and left the question open. Haven't you noticed this kind of thing not only here but also in other places?'

This offensive defence pleased me, and I proceeded to give a straightforward presentation of some of my own ideas on Rilke. As far as Hölderlin and Rilke are concerned, it is absolutely impossible to see them both in the same way, the main reason being the difference in the quality of love in each. One could also substitute the word 'responsibility' for 'love'. Even when Hölderlin soars in the uppermost regions, he still retains responsibility for others in his heart, and this is what eventually unhinged him mentally. But could one find in Rilke a basis for this kind of responsibility?

Heidegger nodded: 'I agree. More detailed work needs to be done on Rilke'. Neither of us had any doubts concerning the significance of the way of being of the poet, as celebrated in Hölderlin's poems, nor about the passion with which Heidegger discusses such a way of being in his treatment of Rilke, and this meant that the conversation proceeded in an even friendlier atmosphere. While I resolved to read 'What Are Poets For?' even more carefully, I was at the same time happy with all Heidegger's responses. We both wanted simply to engage true poetry and understand it. Nor was there the slightest doubt that true poetry comes into closest touch with the time, and the tasks of the time, at points where the contact goes unnoticed.

This was the first half of the conversation during my visit to Heidegger. I then came back to my primary interest and asked him to let me hear his views on the relationship between modern European civilization and Christianity.

Translator's notes

1 INDICATIONS

a. Added to this translation of *Ex oriente lux*. 'Wenn aber die Sprache des Menschen im Wort ist, dann allein ist sie im Lot. Steht sie im Lot, dann winkt ihr die Gewähr der verborgenen Quellen' ('Winke', in *GA* 13:33; emphasis added).

b. Heinrich Wiegand Petzet, *Auf einen Stern zugehen. Begegnungen und Gespräche mit Martin Heidegger 1929–1976* (Frankfurt 1983), especially pp. 80, 175–91, 227.

c. Martin Heidegger, 'Zur Seinsfrage' (*GA* 9), in *Wegmarken* (Frankfurt a.M. 1967), 213–53, 252 (henceforth '*Wm*'); *Identität und Differenz* (Pfullingen 1976), 25; 'Das Wesen der Sprache' (*GA* 12), in *Unterwegs zur Sprache* ['*US*'], 147–204, 187. See also 'Wissenschaft und Besinnung', in *Vorträge und Aufsätze* ['*VA*'] (Pfullingen 1954, 1967), Part 1, 37–62, 39.

d. The original of Hsiao's translation reads: 'Wer kann das Trübe stillend allmählich klären? / 'Wer kann die Ruhe bewegend allmählich beleben?'

e. Heidegger's original reads: 'Wer kann still sein und aus der Stille durch sie auf den Weg bringen (be-wegen) etwas so, dass es zum Erscheinen kommt?'

f. The original reads: 'Wer vermag es, stillend etwas ins Sein zu bringen? / Des Himmels Tao'.

g. An English translation of Buber's *Tschuang-Tse* is now available in Martin Buber, *Chinese Tales*, translated by Alex Page (New Jersey 1991), 1–107. The informative introduction by Irene Eber mentions a typewritten manuscript of a commentary by Buber on the *Laozi* dating from 1924. This is the same year that Richard Wilhelm joined the philosophical faculty at the University of Frankfurt and founded the China Institute there, where he subsequently came into contact with Buber who lived not far away.

h. I am now, of course, persuaded of the importance of raising the question of influence. The bulk of the comparison between *Being and Time* and the classical Daoists in 'Thoughts on the Way' was written before I learned of Heidegger's acquaintance with the Buber edition of the *Zhuangzi* by 1930 (at the latest). The most fascinating aspect of the question of influence in this context concerns the possibility of Heidegger's being acquainted with a translation of the *Zhuangzi before* he wrote *Being and Time*. For more on this issue, see my complementary essay below.

i. *Der Spiegel* 23 (1976), 193–219, 214ff; also in G. Neske and E. Kettering, eds, *Antwort: Martin Heidegger im Gespräch* (Pfullingen 1988), 81–114, 107. Alter and Caputo render '*durch Übernahme von Zen-Buddhismus oder anderen östlichen Welterfahrungen*' as 'because of any takeover by Zen Buddhism or any other Eastern experiences of the world' – a mistranslation that imputes to Zen Buddhism or other Eastern experiences sinister imperialist motives that are absent from Heidegger's remark. For further discussion of this nevertheless strange comment, see the complementary essay.

j. The term translated by 'significant' is '*wegweisend*' – literally: 'way-indicating', with emphasis on the *way* component, and connotations of signposts on the way.

2 THE 'CONVERSATION'

k. The English translation is the first of the texts collected in *On the Way to Language*.

l. One of the few discussions of Kuki Shūzō to have appeared in English is Stephen Light, *Shūzō Kuki and Jean-Paul Sartre* (Carbondale 1987), which also contains translations of some of Kuki's brief essays from the period just before he met Heidegger.

m. Der bislang ungedruckte Text entstand *aus einem Gepräch von der Sprache zwischen einem Japaner und einem Fragenden* 1953/54, veranlasst durch einen Besuch von Prof. Tezuka von der Kaiserlichen Universität Tokio.

n. 'The *nature* of language' here translates 'das *Wesen* der Sprache' in the original. The word *Wesen* is almost a term of art for Heidegger, and is notoriously difficult to translate. 'Being' or 'essence' are other possible translations, though the latter conveys too much of a connotation of essentialism. The discussion is certainly about the 'being' of language, but 'nature' (even with its essentialist connotations) seems more appropriate in this context.

o. Tezuka in his explanatory afterword denies ever having heard Kuki lecture, and suggests that whatever supplementary information about Kuki is presented in Heidegger's text must have come from other Japanese Heidegger had spoken with. He goes on: 'That the visitor from Japan is a keen reader of Heidegger and is familiar with his thinking and ways of expression has nothing to do with me, but rather comes, it seems to me, partly from Heidegger's own motives and his need to write this text. Not only are these specialist ideas and terminology alien to me, but there are also in the text certain expressions which, though not related to a specific idea, I could never have uttered if the visitor from Japan had been me' ('Kaisetsu', 140–1).

p. The words rendered by 'invention' (*Dichtung*) and 'truth' (*Wahrheit*) allude to the title of Goethe's well-known quasi-autobiography, *Dichtung und Wahrheit*.

q. An anomaly here is Heidegger's use of the reading *iro* for the Japanese character designated by *shiki*. In the context of the Buddhist idea of the non-differentiation of *shiki* and *kū*, the character is always read *shiki* rather than *iro*. Since it is highly unlikely that Tezuka would have pronounced it *iro* in his explanation to Heidegger (though he may have mentioned it as an alternative reading in other contexts), one must suppose that Heidegger misread his notes on the discussion and/or that he was later given a reading of the character by another Japanese who was unaware of the Buddhist context.

r. *Benl*: 'Es genügt nicht, [das Geheimnis] nicht zu offenbaren, man darf die anderen gar nicht ahnen lassen, dass man ein Geheimnis besitzt'. *Heidegger*: 'Ein Geheimnis ist erst dann ein Geheimnis, wenn nicht einmal dies zum Vorschein kommt, dass *ein Geheimnis waltet*'.

s. *Benl*: 'Eine Pflaumenblüte / In eine Kirschblüte / Duften und beide / An einem Weidenzweige / Erblühen zu lassen – so wünscht' ich es mir'. *Heidegger*: 'In unserer alten japanischen Dichtung singt ein unbekannter Dichter vom Ineinanderduften der Kirschblüte and Pflaumenblüte am selben Zweig'.

t. Yoneda, *Gespräch und Dichtung* 94–6. The components of *fūga* mean literally something like 'wind-grace', where 'wind' connotes the dynamic life of the natural world. Through attuning themselves to the forces of nature, human beings find themselves naturally inclined to produce songs and poems and other kinds of art. Yoneda also cites remarks by the contemporary Japanese philosopher Tsujimura Kōichi to the effect that Heidegger was 'intensely interested' in Bashō.

u. Again the term translated by 'significant' is 'weg*weisend*'.

3 NOTHING, EMPTINESS, AND THE CLEARING

v. The phrases in question appear as Heidegger's notes in the 1976 (*GA*) edition of 'Was ist Metaphysik?' but not in the English translation by David Krell, 'What Is Metaphysics?', in *BW*. The first reads: '*Nichts und Sein das Selbe*', and the second: '*Nichts als "Sein"*'. 'Die Zeit des Weltbildes', in *Hw* 104. In *Martin Heidegger im Gespräch* Heidegger asks: 'Why do beings have precedence? Why is Nothing not thought as identical with Being?'

w. 'Zur Seinsfrage', 247: 'Das Sein "ist" so wenig wie das Nichts. Aber *Es gibt* beides'.

x. 'Zur Seinsfrage' (Vorwort), in *Wm* 213; see also 239f, 242–4.

y. 'Logos', in *VA* 3:3–25, 25. Compare 'Wozu Dichter?' in *Hw* 250; 'Zur Seinsfrage', in *Wm* 236; *ID* 19; 'Zeit und Sein', in *Zur Sache des Denkens*, 5.

z. Wilhelm, *Laotse* (1911) 89, 4, 45; von Strauss, *Lao-Tse* (1870) 12.

a. A note to the translation of 'What Is Metaphysics?' (by R. F. C. Hull and Alan Crick) in Werner Brock, ed., *Existence and Being* (Chicago 1949), refers the reader to Chapter 40 of the *Laozi*. At the end of the paragraph that ends with the clause '[Dasein] emerges as such existence in each case from the nothing already revealed' (*BW* 105/*Wm* 12), the note reads: 'Cf. "Tao Te Ching" XL: for though all creatures under heaven are products of Being, Being itself is the product of Not-being. Trans.'

b. The *Shinjin-mei* is a poem attributed to the Third Patriarch of Chan Buddhism, Seng-can [Seng-ts'an] (*d*. 606). The *Shōdō-ka* is a poetic work by Yong-jia Xuan-jue [Yung-chia Hsüan-chüeh] (665–713), a Chan master of the school of the Sixth Patriarch.

c. Another feature of Heidegger's conception of Nothing that brings it close to these Mahāyāna Buddhist ideas is the pronounced emphasis in 'What Is Metaphysics?' on the *unity* of *das Nichts* and *das Seiende im Ganzen* (beings in totality): 'Nothingness is encountered in anxiety *together with* beings in totality', (Das Nichts begegnet in der Angst *in eins mit* dem Seienden im Ganzen) (*BW* 104/*Wm* 10; emphasis added); also 'Nothingness rather announces itself *precisely with and in* what-is as it glides away as a whole' (Vielmehr bekundet sich das Nichts *eigens mit und an* dem Seienden als einem entgleitenden im Ganzen) (*BW* 104/*Wm* 11; emphasis added). Remember this was the text that Heidegger noted was 'immediately understood' in Japan when it was first translated.

d. Von Strauss: '. . . *das eine durch das andere erst ist* . . .' Heidegger: 'Das Andere zu ihm [dem Sein] ist nur das Nichts'. . . . 'Sein und Nichts gibt es nicht nebeneinander. Eines verwendet sich für das Andere . . .'

e. *Shinjin-mei*: '*Sein ist nichts anderes als Nichts, / Nichts ist nichts anderes als Sein*'. Heidegger: 'Nichts als "Sein"'; 'Nichts und Sein das Selbe'; 'Sein: Nichts: Selbes'.

f. 'Der Ursprung des Kunstwerkes', in *Hw* 10–11. Compare *FD* 4–6; also 'Das Wesen der Sprache', in *US* 164.

g. *Zhuangzi*: ' . . . *Was den Dingen ihre Dinglichkeit gibt, ist nicht selbst ein Ding.*'
Heidegger: '[Die] Dingheit des Dinges . . . kann selbst nicht wieder ein Ding
sein.' 'Das Sein des Seienden "ist" nicht selbst ein Seiendes.'

h. The Buber translation reads: 'Das, was die Dinge dazu macht, was sie sind,
ist nicht in den Dingen beschränkt' (That which makes things what they are
is not confined in things).

i. Wilhelm, *Laotse* (1911) 13; von Strauss, *Lao-Tse* (1870) 51, 52.

j. The note ('Alētheia – Offenheit – Lichtung, Licht, Leuchten') is appended to
the first appearance of the term *Lichtung*, near the top of *SZ* 133. 'Vom Wesen
der Wahrheit', in *Wm* 96–7. The last two footnotes mentioned are appended
(in the *GA* edition) to the sentence marked by the reference to *Platons Lehre
von der Wahrheit* on *WL* 115/*US* 245; they read: '[*beruht*/has its roots in] rests
in the concealment ('forgetting') of the clearing as such . . . ' and '[truth] put
differently: *unique* development of the unthought *Alētheia* (as clearing) into
truth in the sense of correctness'.

k. There is an echo of this locution, which tightens the connection between the
clearing and Being, when Heidegger writes in the 'Letter on Humanism':
'Nevertheless Being is more "being" [*seiender*] than any being' (*BW* 237/*Wm*
189).

l. 'Das Ende der Philosophie und die Aufgabe des Denkens', in *Zur Seinsfrage*,
73. The English translation has 'opening' for *Lichtung* instead of 'clearing'.

4 *DAO*: WAY AND SAYING

m. The German *Sage* is related, as Heidegger himself remarks, to the Norse *saga*:
'To say, *sagan*, means to show: to let appear, to free luminously-shelteringly
[*lichtend-verbergend frei-geben*] as the extending of what we call World' (*WL*
93/*US* 200). In order to draw attention to the connotations of the poetic, which
are absent from the English 'saying', the word will be translated as 'Saying'.

n. The original reads: 'Vielleicht verbirgt sich im Wort 'Weg', Tao, das Geheimnis
aller Geheimnisse des denkenden Sagens'. Compare Wilhelm's translations of
the characterization, at the end of the first chapter of the *Laozi*, of the unity
of *Sein* and *Nichtsein* in *dao*: 'Diese Einheit ist das Grosse Geheimnis. / Und
des Geheimnisses noch tieferes Geheimnis: / das ist die Pforte der
Offenbarwerdung aller Kräfte' (1911, 3); 'In seiner Einheit heisst es das
Geheimnis. / Des Geheimnisses noch tieferes Geheimnis / ist das Tor, durch
das alle Wunder hervortreten' (1957, 41).

o. We are convinced that, for many reasons having to do with the etymology of
the German term and Heidegger's general usage of it, 'eventuation' would be
a happier rendering of *Ereignis* than the customary 'appropriation'. However,
since it seems better able to convey the play between *ereignen* and *eignen* in
the long quotation from Heidegger that follows in section 3.2 below, we shall
stay with the customary 'appropriation', while distinguishing it by an initial
capital letter from the word's normal usage.

p. It is impossible to convey Heidegger's plays on the relations between *denken*
and *dichten* in an elegant translation. The verb *dichten* means to compose in
the medium of language, and has connotations – through *dicht*, meaning
'dense', or 'thick' – of condensing; but it seems best to bring out the connection with *Dichtung* ('poetry') while retaining the verbal sense of *dichten*.
'Poetizing' should simply be taken as shorthand for 'composing poetry', or
'writing works of literature'.

q. '*Das Regende im Zeigen der Sage ist das Eignen*' (italics in original).

r. Rüdenberg/Stange, *Chinesisch–Deutsches Wörterbuch* (Hamburg 1924, ³1963),
476, no. 6062; also Morohashi, *Dai kan-wa jiten,* no. 39010, II.1.

s. A footnote on this page of Wilhelm's introduction reads: 'In Chinese translations of the Bible, *logos* is almost always rendered as *dao*'. And a few lines later he writes: 'Used as a verb, the word [*dao*] means "to speak" [*reden*] or "to say" [*sagen*] . . .'

t. 'Wort – die verlautende Sage' ('Der Weg zur Sprache', *GA* 12:253). The note is appended to the phrase 'The origin of the word' (*WL* 133) / 'In der ereignisartigen Herkunft des Wortes' (*US* 265).

5 A KIND OF CONFESSION

u. *Weite* is a favorite term of the later Heidegger: in *Gelassenheit* the 'realm' [*Gegnet*] is referred to as '*die freie Weite*' and as '*Weile* and *Weite* at the same time'; and when things are going well, they 'rest in the return to the staying [*Weile*] of the farness [*Weite*] of their belonging together' (*DT* 66–7/*G* 39–41; see also 75–6/52).

v. The text of this lecture is published in *GA* 59 (Frankfurt a.M. 1993).

w. The German title of the lecture course in question is 'Phänomenologie der Anschauung und des Ausdrucks'. Heidegger has his 'Japanese' bring up the course and the transcript that found its way to Japan, estimating the date as '1921' and saying: 'The title, if I am not mistaken, was "Expression and Appearance" [Ausdruck und Erscheinung]' (*WL* 6/*US* 91). The Inquirer responds by saying: 'That was in any case the theme of the course'. In a later exchange the Inquirer says to his interlocutor: 'The lecture "Expression and Appearance" (or was the title not rather "Expression and Meaning [*Bedeutung*]"?) was fairly polemical . . .' (34/128). See also the further discussions (35–9/129–34) of the topics of expression and appearance.

According to Tsujimura Kōichi (in a speech on the occasion of Heidegger's sixtieth birthday), the first Japanese to study with Heidegger, Yamanouchi Tokuryū, went to Germany in 1921 (*JH* 159–65, 159).

x. The relevant passage in the Buber edition, which comes right after the discussion of what 'makes things things', reads: 'Tao ist die Schranke des Schrankenlosen, die Schrankenlosigkeit des Beschränkten' (*Dao* is the limit of the limitless, the limitlessness of the limited). Stange has: 'Aber die Grenze des Unbegrenzten ist eben Unbegrenztheit der Grenzen.'

6 CONCLUSIONS

y. Hsiao writes that he was quite ambivalent about resuming the collaboration with Heidegger the following summer. While, on the one hand, 'a *Laozi* by Heidegger would create a great sensation in the world of philosophy. . . . On the other hand, I was slightly perturbed during the collaboration by a feeling that perhaps Heidegger's notes could be going beyond what is afforded by a straight translation' (*EMH* 126).

z. The Wilhelm translation makes it clear that the answer to the question 'Who?' is 'the accomplished sages of old'.

a. The Wilhelm translation of the lines from *Laozi* 15 discussed above reads: 'Wer kann (wie sie) das Trübe durch Stille allmählich klären? / Wer kann (wie sie) die Ruhe durch Dauer allmählich erzeugen? (where the *sie* refers to the masters of old.) In *Gelassenheit* the discussion turns at one point to the extent to which 'rest [*Ruhe*] is the seat and rule of all movement [*Bewegung*]' (*DT* 67/*G* 41; *GA* 13:51).

b. Hsiao writes: 'Lao-tse's conception of *wu*, Nothing, and his aversion to any kind of rationalism corresponded to Heidegger's ideas' (*EMH* 127). He goes on to say that, in response to his own remark to the effect that 'the Chinese of [Laozi's] time were not acquainted with Aristotelian logic', Heidegger 'spontaneously' remarked: 'Thank God the Chinese weren't acquainted with it' (*EMH* 128).

c. The author is here playing on a locution of Heidegger's in 'Hölderlin's Earth and Heaven', which speaks of 'the preserved greatness of [the] beginning' of the European tradition [*dem gesparten Grossen seines Anfangs*], by writing of 'das Aus*gesparte* des *Grossen*' – the gaps, or lacunae, in the greatness.

7 TEZUKA TOMIO, 'AN HOUR WITH HEIDEGGER': TRANSLATION

d. In the original edition of *Ex oriente lux*, Tezuka's Japanese text was published on the left-hand page, with Reinhard May's translation on the facing right. The present translation was made by translating Dr May's German translation and then revising the English version, where advisable, in the light of the Japanese original. My thanks to Setsuko Aihara for her assistance with this latter phase of the procedure. I have also consulted the translation by Elmar Weinmayr in *JH*, 173–9. Dr May informs me that there is a third translation, by Yoshiko Oshima, in Florian Vetsch, *Martin Heidegger's Angang der interkulturellen Auseinandersetzung* (Würzburg 1992).

e. The portion of Tezuka's report for the *Tōkyō Shinbun* concerning Heidegger is reprinted just after the 'Kaisetsu' to Tezuka's translation of the 'Conversation' (pp. 151–3). Tezuka recounts how impressed he was at the way Christianity seemed to provide 'a kind of unconscious, spiritual foundation for everyday life' on the part of the Europeans. Though he does not actually use the term, he is concerned about the *nihilism* of the Japanese in the post-War era, for whom 'there is no support for their life corresponding to Christianity in Europe'. He ends his account of this to Heidegger with the statement: 'We Japanese currently find ourselves in a state of great confusion'. (The Heidegger portion of Tezuka's report is translated into German by Elmar Weinmayr in *JH* 179–80.)

f. The original reads:

> Hibari yori
> ue ni yasurau
> tōge kana.

Elmar Weinmayr points out in a note to his translation at this point that the unnamed subject of the 'quietly resting' could be either the mountain pass towering high above the poet, who is going to climb it, or else the poet himself, who has already climbed it and is now – almost one with it from his exertions – resting on it himself (*JH* 174).

g. This clause appears at the beginning of the concluding paragraph of Heidegger's essay (*PLT* 142, *Hw* 295).

Glossary of Chinese and Japanese characters

(in alphabetical order of the words in romanization)

CHINESE

dao	道
dao fa zi ran	道法自然
fa	法
ming	明
sheng	生
wan wu	萬物
wu	無
xiang sheng	相生
yu	有

JAPANESE

ba (ha)	葉
fūga	風雅
iki	いき
iro	色
kotoba	言葉
kū	空
kū mu	空無
shiki (iro)	色
shiki soku ze kū	色即是空
sora	空
yūgen	幽玄

PROPER NAMES AND BOOK TITLES

Laozi	老子
Ōhazama Shūei	大峽秀栄
Tezuka Tomio	手塚富雄
Wang Bi	王弼
Zhuangzi	莊子
Dao De Jing	道徳經
Shinjin-mei	信心銘
Shōdō-ka	證道歌
Haideggā to no ichijikan	「ハイデッガーとの一時間」
Kotoba ni tsuite no taiwa	「ことばについての対話」
Zhiang Xi-Jang	蒋錫昌

Bibliography

Edition numbers are indicated in superscript preceding the year of publication.

1 HEIDEGGER'S TEXTS

'Aus der Erfahrung des Denkens' (1947). In *Gesamtausgabe (GA)*, vol. 13. Frankfurt a.M.: Vittorio Klostermann, 1983, pp. 75–86.

'Aus einem Gespräch von der Sprache' (1953/4). In *Unterwegs zur Sprache (US)*, Pfullingen: Günther Neske, 1959, ^{5}1975, pp. 83–155. Also in *GA*, vol. 12 (1985), pp. 79–146.

'Aletheia' (1943). In *Vorträge und Aufsätze (VA)*, Part I. Pfullingen: Günther Neske, 1954, ^{3}1967, pp. 53–78.

'Brief an Herrn Hsiao' (9 Oct. 1947). In *Heidegger and Asian Thought*. Edited by Graham Parkes. Honolulu: University of Hawaii Press, 1987, p. 102.

'Brief an W. J. Richardson' (1962). In William J. Richardson, *Heidegger: Through Phenomenology to Thought*. The Hague: Martinus Nijhoff, 1963, ^{3}1974, pp. ix–xxiii.

'Brief über den "Humanismus"' (1946). Bern: Francke 1947, ^{3}1975, pp. 53–119. In *Wegmarken (Wm)*. Frankfurt a.M.: Vittorio Klostermann, 1967, pp. 145–94. Also in *GA*, vol. 9 (1976), pp. 313–64.

'Briefwechsel mit einem japanischen Kollegen' (1963). In *Begegnung. Zeitschrift für Literatur, Bildende Kunst, Musik und Wissenschaft*. 1965, pp. 2–7.

'Das Ding' (1950). In *VA*, Part II. Pfullingen: Günther Neske, 1954, ^{3}1967, pp. 37–55.

'Das Ende der Philosophie und die Aufgabe des Denkens' (1964, 1966). In *Zur Sache des Denkens*. Tübingen: Max Niemeyer, 1969, ^{2}1976, pp. 61–80.

'Das Wesen der Sprache' (1957/8). In *Unterwegs zur Sprache (US)*, Pfullingen: Günther Neske, 1959, ^{5}1975, pp. 157–216. Also in *GA*, vol. 12 (1985), pp. 147–204.

'Der Spruch des Anaximander' (1946). In *Holzwege (Hw)*, Frankfurt a.M.: Vittorio Klostermann, ^{5}1972, pp. 296–343. Also in *GA*, vol. 5 (1977), pp. 321–373.

'Der Ursprung des Kunstwerkes' (1935/6). In *Hw*, pp. 7–68. Also in *GA*, vol. 5, pp. 1–74.

'Der Weg zur Sprache' (1959). In *US*. Pfullingen: Günther Neske, 1959, ^{5}1975, pp. 239–68. Also in *GA*, vol. 12 (1985), pp. 227–57.

Die Frage nach dem Ding. Zu Kants Lehre von den transzendentalen Grundsätzen (1935/6). Tübingen: Max Niemeyer, 1962. Also in *GA*, vol. 41 (1984).

'Die Kehre' (1949). In *Die Technik und die Kehre*. Pfullingen: Günther Neske, 1962, pp. 37–47.

'Die Sprache' (1950, 1951, 1959). In *US*. Pfullingen: Günther Neske, 1959, [5]1975, pp. 9–33. Also in *GA*, vol. 12 (1985), pp. 7–30.
'Die Zeit des Weltbildes' (1938). In *Hw*, pp. 69–104. Also in *GA*, vol. 5 (1977), pp. 75–113.
Einführung in die Metaphysik (1935). Tübingen: Max Niemeyer, 1953, [3]1966. Also in *GA*, vol. 40 (1983).
'Einleitung zu "Was ist Metaphysik?"' (1949). In *Wm*, pp. 195–212. Also in *GA*, vol. 9 (1976), pp. 365–83.
'Grundsätze des Denkens' (1958). In *Jahrbuch für Psychologie und Psychotherapie* 6, 1958, pp. 33–41.
'Hölderlins Erde und Himmel' (1959). In *Hölderlin-Jahrbuch* 11, 1958–60, pp. 17–39.
Identität und Differenz (1957). Pfullingen: Günther Neske, [5]1976.
'Logos' (1951). In *VA*, Part III. Pfullingen: Günther Neske, 1954, [3]1967, pp. 3–25.
'Martin Heidegger im Gespräch' (The television interview, 1969). In *Martin Heidegger im Gespräch*. Edited by Richard Wisser. Freiburg/Munich: 1970, pp. 67–77.
'Nachwort. Ein Brief an einen jungen Studenten' (1950). In *VA*, Part II. Pfullingen: Günther Neske, 1954, [3]1967, pp. 56–9.
'Nachwort zu "Was ist Metaphysik?"' (1943). In *Wm*, pp. 99–108. Also in *GA*, vol. 9 (1976), pp. 303–12.
Sein und Zeit (1927). Tübingen: Max Niemeyer, [11]1967. Also in *GA*, vol. 2 (1977).
'Seminar in Le Thor' (1969). In *Seminare*. *GA*, vol. 15 (1986), pp. 326–71.
'Spiegel-Gespräch mit Martin Heidegger' (1966). *Der Spiegel*. No. 23, 1976, pp. 193–219. Also in *Antwort. Martin Heidegger im Gespräch*. Edited by G. Neske and E. Kettering. Pfullingen: Günther Neske, 1988, pp. 81–114.
'Überwindung der Metaphysik' (1936–46)/(1951). In *VA*, Part I. Pfullingen: Günther Neske, 1954, [3]1967, pp. 63–91.
'Vom Wesen der Wahrheit' (1930/43, [2]1949). In *Wm*, pp. 73–98. Also in *GA*, vol. 9 (1976), pp. 177–202.
'Vorbemerkung' (1967). In *Wm*. *GA*, vol. 9 (1976), pp. ix–x.
'Vorwort zu ersten Ausgabe der "Frühen Schriften"' (1972). In *GA*, vol. 1 (1978), pp. 55–7.
Was heisst Denken?(1951/2, 1952). Tübingen: Günther Neske, 1954, [4]1984.
'Was heisst Denken?' (1952). In *VA*, Part II. Pfullingen: Günther Neske, 1954, [3]1967, pp. 3–17.
'Was ist Metaphysik?' (1929). In *Wm*. *GA*, vol. 9 (1976), pp. 103–22.
'Wissenschaft und Besinnung' (1953). In *VA*, Part I. Pfullingen: Günther Neske, 1954, [3]1967, pp. 37–62.
'Wozu Dichter?' (1946). In *Hw*. *GA*, vol. 5 (1977), pp. 269–320.
'Zeit und Sein' (1962). In *Zur Sache des Denkens*. Tübingen: Max Niemeyer, 1969, [2]1976, pp. 1–25.
'Zur Erörterung der Gelassenheit' (1944/5). In *Aus der Erfahrung des Denkens*. *GA*, vol. 13 (1983), pp. 37–74.
'Zur Seinsfrage' (1955, 1956), In *Wm*, pp. 213–54. Also in *GA*, vol. 9 (1976), pp. 385–426.

2   HEIDEGGER'S TEXTS IN ENGLISH TRANSLATION

Basic Writings. Edited by David Farrell Krell. New York: Harper & Row, 1977.
Being and Time. Translated by John Macquarrie and Edward Robinson. New York: Harper & Row, 1962.
Discourse on Thinking. Translated by John M. Anderson and E. Hans Freund. New York: Harper Torchbooks, 1966.

Early Greek Thinking. Translated by David Farrell Krell and Frank A. Capuzzi. New York: Harper & Row, 1975.
Identity and Difference. Translated by Joan Stambaugh. New York: Harper & Row, 1969.
An Introduction to Metaphysics. Translated by Ralph Mannheim. New Haven: Yale University Press, 1959.
On the Way to Language. Translated by Peter D. Hertz. New York: Harper & Row, 1971.
'Only a God Can Save Us'. *Der Spiegel*'s interview with Martin Heidegger (1966). Translated by Maria P. Alter and John D. Caputo. In *The Heidegger Controversy: A Critical Reader.* Edited by Richard Wolin. Cambridge/London: MIT Press, 1993.
Poetry, Language and Thought. Translated by Albert Hofstadter. New York: Harper & Row, 1971.
The Question Concerning Technology and Other Essays. Translated by William Lovitt. New York: Harper & Row, 1977.
'Preface' (by Heidegger) to: William J. Richardson, *Heidegger: Through Phenomenology to Thought.* The Hague: Martinus Nijhoff, 1963.
Time and Being. Translated by Joan Stambaugh. New York: Harper & Row, 1972.
What is a Thing? Translated by W. B. Barton, Jr and Vera Deutsch, with an analysis by Eugene T. Gendlin. Chicago: H. Regnery Co., 1968.
What is Called Thinking? Translated by J. Glenn Gray. New York: Harper & Row, 1968.

3   EAST ASIAN TEXTS (SOURCE TEXTS IN GERMAN TRANSLATION)

Zhuangzi (Chuang Tzu)

Reden und Gleichnisse des Tschuang-Tse. Edited and translated by Martin Buber. Leipzig: 1910.
Dschuang Dsï [Chuang Tzu]. Das wahre Buch vom südlichen Blütenland. Translated with commentary by Richard Wilhelm [Jena: 1912]. Düsseldorf/Cologne: 1972.
Tschuang-Tse. Dichtung und Weisheit. Aus dem chinesischen Urtext übersetzt von Hans O. H. Stange. Leipzig: 1936.

Laozi (Lao Tzu)

Lao-Tse, Tao Tê King. Translated with commentary by Victor von Strauss [Leipzig: 1870]. Zürich: 1959.
Laotse: Tao te king. Das Buch des Alten vom Sinn und Leben. Translated with a commentary by Richard Wilhelm [Jena: 1911]. Düsseldorf/Cologne: 1957, 1972.
Lao Tse: Tao Te King. Das Buch vom rechten Wege und von der rechten Gesinnung. Translated with introduction and commentary by Jan Ulenbrook. Frankfurt a.M.: 1980.

Zen Buddhism

Zen. Der lebendige Buddhismus in Japan. Texts selected and translated by Schuej Ōhasama [Ōhazama Shūei]. Edited by August Faust, with preface by Rudolf Otto. Gotha/Stuttgart: 1925.

4 SECONDARY LITERATURE

Monographs (including dictionaries)

Biemel, Walter. *Heidegger*. Reinbek bei Hamburg: 1973.

Borsche, Tilman. *Sprachansichten: Der Begriff der menschlichen Rede in der Sprachphilosophie Wilhelm von Humboldts*. Stuttgart: 1981.

Chang Chung-yuan. *Tao: A New Way of Thinking. A Translation of the Tao Te Ching with an Introduction and Commentaries*. New York: 1975.

Ch'en Ku-Ying. *Lao Tzu. Text, Notes and Comments*. Translated and adapted by Rhett Y. W. Young and Roger T. Ames. San Francisco: 1977.

Cho, Kah Kyung. *Bewusstsein und Natursein: Phänomenologischer West-Ost-Diwan*. Freiburg/Munich: 1987.

Hempel, Hans-Peter. *Heidegger und Zen*. Frankfurt a.M.: 1987.

Herrmann, Friedrich Wilhelm von. *Die Selbstinterpretation Martin Heideggers*. Meisenheim aG: 1964.

—— *Hermeneutische Phänomenologie des Daseins. Eine Erläuterung von 'Sein und Zeit'*, vol. 1. Frankfurt a.M.: 1987.

Hisamatsu, Hōseki Shin'ichi. *Die Fülle des Nichts. Vom Wesen des Zen. Eine systematische Erläuterung*. Translated by Takashi Hirata and Johanna Fischer. Pfullingen: ²1980.

Hsia, Adrian (ed.). *Deutsche Denker über China*. Frankfurt a.M.: 1985.

Humboldt, Wilhelm von. 'Über die Verschiedenheit des menschlichen Sprachbaues und ihren Einfluss auf die geistige Entwicklung des Menschengeschlechts [1830–1835].' In *Wilhelm von Humboldt, Schriften zur Sprachphilosophie*, vol. III. Edited by Flitner/Giel. Darmstadt: 1963, pp. 368–756. (Akademie Edition: vol. VII, pp. 1–344.)

Löwith, Karl. *Heidegger. Denker in dürftiger Zeit*. Göttingen: 1953, ²1965.

Morohashi, Tetsuji. *Dai kan-wa jiten* [Chinese–Japanese dictionary] 13 vols. Tokyo: 1986.

Nakamura, Hajime. *Ways of Thinking of Eastern Peoples: India–China–Tibet–Japan*. Honolulu: 1964, ⁵1971.

Needham, Joseph. *Science and Civilization in China*, vol. 2. Cambridge: 1956, ⁴1975.

Nishitani Keiji. *Was ist Religion?* Frankfurt a.M.: 1982.

Okutsu, H. *Neues Japanisch-Deutsches Wörterbuch*. Tokyo: 1959, 1982.

Parkes, Graham (ed.). *Heidegger and Asian Thought*. Honolulu: 1987.

Petzet, Heinrich Wiegand. *Auf einen Stern zugehen. Begegnungen und Gespräche mit Martin Heidegger 1929-1976*. Frankfurt a.M.: 1983.

Pöggeler, Otto. *Der Denkweg Martin Heideggers*. Pfullingen: 1963, 1983.

Rüdenberg/Stange. *Chinesisch-Deutsches Wörterbuch*. Hamburg: 1924, ³1963.

Saner, Hans. *Jaspers*. Reinbek bei Hamburg: 1970.

Schelling, Friedrich Wilhelm Joseph von. 'Philosophie der Mythologie' (1842). In *Ausgewählte Schriften* vol. 6, Part 2. Frankfurt a.M.: 1985.

Waldenfels, Hans. *Absolutes Nichts. Zur Grundlegung des Dialogs zwischen Buddhismus und Christentum*. Freiburg: 1976, ³1980.

Wang Pi. *Commentary on the Lao Tzu*. Translated by Ariane Rump. Honolulu: 1979.

Wieger, León, S. J. *Chinese Characters. Their Origin, Etymology, History, Classification and Signification. A Thorough Study from Chinese Documents* (1915). Translated by L. Davrout, S. J. Reprint. New York: 1965.

Yoneda, Michiko. *Gespräch und Dichtung. Ein Auseinandersetzungsversuch der Sprachauffassung Heideggers mit einem japanischen Sagen*. Frankfurt a.M./Berne/New York: 1984.

Articles

Barrett, William. 'Zen for the West'. Introduction to D. T. Suzuki, *Zen Buddhism*. Garden City, NY: 1956, pp. vii–xx.

Benl, Oscar. 'Seami Motokiyo und der Geist des Nō-Schauspiels: Geheime kunst-kritische Schriften aus dem 15. Jahrhundert.' In *Akademie der Wissenschaften und der Literatur, Abhandlungen der Klasse der Literatur*, Jahrgang 1952, no. 5. Wiesbaden: 1953, pp. 103–249.

Biemel, Walter. 'Dichtung und Sprache bei Heidegger'. *Man and World*. Vol. 2, no. 4, 1969, pp. 487–514.

Chang Chung-yuan. 'Reflections'. In *Erinnerung an Martin Heidegger (EMH)*. Edited by Günther Neske. Pfullingen: 1977, pp. 65–70.

—— 'Tao: A New Way of Thinking'. In *Journal of Chinese Philosophy*. Vol. 1, 1974, pp. 137–52.

—— 'The Philosophy of Taoism according to Chuang Tzu'. *Philosophy East and West*. Vol. 27, 1977, pp. 409–22.

Chen, Ellen Marie. 'The Origin and Development of Being (*Yu*) from Non-Being (*Wu*) in the *Tao Te Ching*'. In *International Philosophical Quarterly*. Vol. 13, 1973, pp. 403–17.

Cheng Chung-Ying. 'Remarks on the Ontological and Transontological Foundations of Language'. In *Journal of Chinese Studies*. Vol. 5, 1978, pp. 335–40.

Fischer-Barnicol, Hans A. 'Spiegelungen – Vermittlungen'. In *EMH*, pp. 87–103.

Fu, Charles Wei-Hsun. 'Creative Hermeneutics: Taoist Metaphysics and Heidegger'. In *Journal of Chinese Philosophy*. Vol. 3, 1976, pp. 115–43.

Hakoishi, Masayuki. 'Die Phänomenologie in Japan'. In *Zeitschrift für Philosophische Forschung*. Vol. 37, 1983, pp. 299–315.

Heim, Michael. 'A Philosophy of Comparison: Heidegger and Lao Tzu'. In *Journal of Chinese Philosophy*. Vol. 11, 1984, pp. 307–35.

Hirsch, Elisabeth Feist. 'Martin Heidegger and the East'. In *Philosophy East and West*. Vol. 20, 1970, pp. 247–63.

Hsiao, Paul Shih-yi. 'Heidegger and Our Translation of the *Tao Te Ching*'. In *HAT*, pp. 93–101.

—— 'Laotse und die Technik'. In *Die Katholischen Missionen*. Vol. 75, 1956, pp. 72–4.

—— 'Wir trafen uns am Holzmarktplatz'. In *EMH*, pp. 119–29.

Jung, Hwa Yol. 'Heidegger's Way with Sinitic Thinking'. In *HAT*, pp. 217–44.

Lohmann, Johannes. 'Der Sophismus des Kung-Sun Lung (zur ontologischen Amphibolie des Chinesischen)'. In *Lexis* 2, 1949, pp. 3–11.

Nagley, Winfield E. 'Introduction to the Symposium and Reading of a Letter from Martin Heidegger'. In *PEW*. Vol. 20, 1970, p. 221.

Nishida, Kitarō. 'Die morgenländischen und abendländischen Kulturformen in alter Zeit vom metaphysischen Standpunkt aus gesehen'. In *Abhandlungen der preussischen Akademie der Wissenschaften*. Vol. 19, Berlin: 1939.

Parkes, Graham. 'Afterwords–Language'. In *HAT*, pp. 213–16.

—— 'Dōgen/Heidegger/Dōgen: A Review of Dōgen Studies'. In *PEW*. Vol. 37, 1987, pp. 437–54.

—— 'Thoughts on the Way: *Being and Time* via Lao-Chuang'. In *HAT*, pp. 105–44.

—— 'Introduction'. In *HAT*, pp. 1–14.

Petzet, Heinrich Wiegand. 'Die Bremer Freunde'. In *EMH*, pp. 179–90.

Pöggeler, Otto. 'Sein als Ereignis'. In *Zeitschrift für Philosophische Forschung*. Vol. 13, 1959, pp. 597–632.

—— 'West–East Dialogue: Heidegger and Lao-tzu'. In *HAT*. Edited by Graham Parkes, pp. 47–78.

'Prajñā-pāramitā-hṛdaya-sūtra'. In *Buddhist Mahāyāna Texts*, Part II. In *The Sacred Books of the East*. Edited by F. Max Müller. Vol. 49, pp. 147–9, 153–4.

Schirmacher, Wolfgang. 'Gelassenheit bei Schopenhauer und bei Heidegger'. In *Schopenhauer Jahrbuch*. Vol. 63, 1982, pp. 54–66.

Smith, Carl T. 'A Heideggerian Interpretation of the Way of Lao Tzu'. In *Ching Feng*. Vol. 10, 1967, pp. 5–19.

Stambaugh, Joan. 'Heidegger, Taoism and the Question of Metaphysics'. In *Journal of Chinese Philosophy*. Vol. 11, 1984, pp. 337–52.

Tezuka Tomio. 'Haideggā to no ichi jikan' ('An Hour with Heidegger'). In *Kotoba ni tsuite no taiwa* ('From a Conversation on Language'). *Haideggā zenshū* Vol. 21. Tokyo: 1968, ³1975, pp. 159–66.

—— 'Kaisetsu'. *Haideggā zenshū*. Vol. 21. Tokyo: 1969, ³1975, pp. 137–50.

Tsujimura Kōichi. 'Die Seinsfrage und das absolute Nichts-Erwachen – In memoriam Martin Heidegger'. In *Transzendenz und Immanenz*. Stuttgart: 1977, pp. 289–301.

—— 'Martin Heidegger im Zeugnis von Kōichi Tsujimura'. In *Martin Heidegger im Gespräch*. Edited by Richard Wisser. Freiburg/Munich: 1970, pp. 27–30.

Tugendhat, Ernst. 'Das Sein und das Nichts'. In *Durchblicke – Martin Heidegger zum 80. Geburtstag*. Frankfurt a.M.: 1970, pp. 132–61.

Ueda, Shizuteru. 'Die zen-buddhistische Erfahrung des Wahr-Schönen'. In *Eranos Jahrbuch*. Vol. 53, 1984, pp. 197–240.

Uhsadel, Walter. 'Rezension: Heidegger, Martin: *Unterwegs zur Sprache*.' In *Theologische Literaturzeitung*. Vol. 3, 1961, pp. 217–21.

Rising sun over Black Forest
Heidegger's Japanese connections

Graham Parkes[1]

Reinhard May has argued on the basis of close textual comparisons that Heidegger's formulations of his major thoughts on Being, Nothing, the clearing, and on the complex relations between language, Way, and Saying, were influenced by his readings of German translations of Daoist and Zen texts and his collaboration with Paul Shih-yi Hsiao on translating selected chapters from the *Laozi*. Since Heidegger was so reticent about his acquaintance with East Asian ideas, it is hard to determine when he first started reading in that area. While it is likely, given the intellectual milieu in which he grew up, that this acquaintance came early, the first confirmed instance so far is Petzet's report of Heidegger's consulting the Buber edition of the *Zhuangzi* in 1930, an event that indicates a prior familiarity with that text.[2] This revelation should not perhaps have come as a major surprise in view of Heidegger's general reticence with respect to the sources of his ideas.[3] Some good treatments of the early phases of his intellectual biography work have appeared recently in the secondary literature in English, though the scholarship continues to ignore extra-European sources or influences.[4] A significant feature, it seems to me, in Heidegger's philosophical development, which is mentioned but not elaborated by Reinhard May, is the contact he enjoyed during the 1920s with several of the best minds in modern Japanese philosophy. The present essay aims, as a complement to the preceding discussion of Heidegger's hidden sources, to sketch some relevant background for readers unacquainted with Japanese thought, and in particular to convey a sense of the major figures in this context: Tanabe Hajime, Nishida Kitarō, and Kuki Shūzō.

If I may be permitted an autobiographical remark: before learning of Heidegger's familiarity with Buber's *Zhuangzi*, I wrote an essay outlining the Daoist themes to be found in *Sein und Zeit* and suggesting some kind of 'pre-established harmony' between Heidegger's thought and Daoist ideas.[5] Reinhard May has noted that the Buber edition was first published in 1910, and that the other texts with which Heidegger is known to have been familiar date from around that period or earlier: Von Strauss' *Lao-Tse* (1870) and Wilhelm's *Laotse* (1911). It now seems probable that (at least some of) the parallels with Daoist ideas derive from Heidegger's familiarity with the *Zhuangzi* from the time during which *Sein und Zeit* was being written. It is moreover likely, as I suggest below, that his acquaintance with Zen texts also dates from this period.

Two more general considerations tend to support the suggestion that Heidegger may have been influenced early in his career by East Asian ideas. First, with the publication of *Being and Time* in 1927, he inaugurated the most powerful 'destruction' of the Western metaphysical tradition since Nietzsche – several years after becoming acquainted with ideas from a quite alien yet sophisticated philosophical tradition that had been quite *un*metaphysical throughout most of its history. Second, the enormous enthusiasm for Heidegger's ideas in East Asian philosophical circles, and the fact that his later thinking has so many patent affinities (some of which he himself acknowledges) with East Asian thought, suggest some kind of prior harmony. In view of the conclusions drawn by Reinhard May, one is forced to entertain the possibility that this harmony may have been occasioned by some quiet appropriation on Heidegger's part. Whereas the main text above lays major emphasis on Chinese works, what follows below will focus more on Japanese thinkers.

* * *

In 1921 Kuki Shūzō, the 33-year-old scion of a well-to-do aristocratic family, whose father, Baron Kuki, was director of the Imperial Museum in Tokyo, went to Europe to study philosophy. A man of unusually subtle intelligence, Kuki lived in Germany and France for eight years. From 1922 to 1923 he studied neo-Kantianism with Heinrich Rickert in Heidelberg. Possessing the means to do things properly, Kuki had Rickert give him private tutorials on Kant's first *Critique*.[6] He then went to Paris, where he visited Bergson (good taste being a salient feature of Kuki's personality). He was, in any case, a thinker of fine aesthetic sensibilities, who had grown up in a quintessentially Japanese milieu, in an atmosphere of elegance and excellence: in his youth he had benefited from the beneficent tutelage of the well-known art critic and scholar Okakura Kakuzō.[7] During his time in Paris, Kuki wrote a draft of his best-known work, *'Iki' no kōzō* (*The Structure of 'iki'*); and when he left France in 1927, it was for Freiburg, to study phenomenology with Husserl – at whose home he would meet a young *Dozent* by the name of Martin Heidegger.

Another Japanese philosopher of note, Yamanouchi Tokuryū, went to study in Europe in 1921, as the first of several soon-to-be-eminent thinkers from Japan to make 'the Freiburg pilgrimage' to study with Husserl (and then Heidegger).[8] The same age as Heidegger, Yamanouchi was a scholar of broad range who was one of the first to introduce phenomenology to Japan and would later initiate the formal study of Greek philosophy at Kyoto University. At Kyoto he had as a teacher and then senior colleague Nishida Kitarō (1870–1945), a thinker whose epoch-making work *Zen no kenkyū* (*An Inquiry into the Good*) of 1911 is regarded as the first master-piece of modern Japanese philosophical thought.[9] Later, during the 1930s, Yamanouchi was to become one of the few thinkers of sufficient stature to challenge Nishida's formidable philosophical system.[10]

The following year two more visitors – men destined to become major figures in modern Japanese philosophy – arrived in Germany: Tanabe Hajime and Miki Kiyoshi. Both were younger colleagues of 'the Master', Nishida. Miki went first to Heidelberg to work with Heinrich Rickert, and thence to Marburg to study with Heidegger after the latter's move there in late 1923.[11] Tanabe went to Berlin to work with Alois Riehl, but soon moved to Freiburg to study with Husserl. In Freiburg he was introduced to Heidegger who, though four years his junior, impressed him as brilliant. Since one sometimes hears of the 'Chinese and Japanese students' who studied with Heidegger over the years, it should be noted that neither Tanabe nor Kuki was a mere student when Heidegger made their acquaintance. Tanabe had already published two substantial books, in the philosophy of science and philosophy of mathematics (1915 and 1918), and Kuki, who was a year older than Heidegger, had spent the previous six years studying philosophy with several of the great minds of the time.

Japanese commentators sometimes characterize in broad strokes the major difference between the philosophy of the so-called Kyoto School and the mainstream of the Western philosophical tradition by saying that, whereas European thought tends towards philosophies of life based upon inquiry into the nature of being, East Asian philosophies tend to lay greater emphasis on the topics of death and nothingness. This general-ization can provide a preliminary orientation that is by no means misleading, especially since what makes Heidegger's *Being and Time* such a revolutionary work is the central place it accords to *das Nichts*, as well as the 'existential conception' of death developed there – as confirmed by the crucial role these ideas play in Heidegger's subsequent pursuit of the 'question of Being'. It is thus an extremely interesting question to what extent Heidegger had already developed his ideas on nothingness and death by the time of his first contact with the ideas of the Kyoto School.

TANABE HAJIME AND A PHILOSOPHY OF DEATH

Tanabe Hajime is widely regarded as being the second greatest figure (after Nishida) in modern Japanese philosophy and has been taken to be the 'founder' of the Kyoto School.[12] His personal and philosophical rela-tionship with Heidegger was much closer and more enduring than Miki's, who became sharply critical of his former mentor after the events of 1933.[13] It was in part because of Nishida's interest in phenomenology that Tanabe had gone to Freiburg to study with Husserl.[14] But his enthusiasm over the new turn the method was taking at the hands of Heidegger prompted Tanabe to attend the lecture course the younger thinker gave in the summer semester of 1923 under the title 'Ontology: Hermeneutics of Facticity'. Heidegger had, in turn, ample occasion to be impressed by the visitor from Japan, having gladly acceded to his request for private tutorials in German philosophy.[15] Over the ensuing decades the two men remained on cordial terms, and when Tanabe was awarded (*in absentia*) an honorary doctorate by the University of Freiburg, Heidegger sent him a congratulatory copy of the limited edition of his *Gespräch mit Hebel* together with a recent photograph.[16]

An appraisal of the nature of the philosophical interchange between Tanabe and Heidegger is hindered by the almost complete silence the latter maintained about his Japanese colleagues and their ideas. And while Tanabe continued to refer to Heidegger's works throughout his career, he was a reticent man and much of his correspondence has been lost or destroyed. However, approaching from the side of Tanabe's references to Heidegger, let us see what reconstruction of their philosophical relationship is possible – first with respect to the topic of death and then to the idea of nothingness.

After his return to Japan in 1924, Tanabe published his essay 'A New Turn in Phenomenology: Heidegger's Phenomenology of Life', the first substantial commentary on his thought to be published in any language.[17] The essay is of particular interest since its concluding section gives us an idea of how Heidegger's 1923 lecture course ended. (The transcript published in the *Gesamtausgabe* is said by the editor to be lacking the last page or two: 'it breaks off suddenly in the middle of the train of thought'.)[18] Missing from the transcript in the *Gesamtausgabe* – but prominent in the conclusion of Tanabe's discussion of Heidegger's phenomenology of life – is an account of the role played by the confrontation with death in the attainment of self-understanding.

> Just as life is not merely a passage [of time], so death is not the mere termination or breaking off of such a passage. Rather death stands before *Dasein* as something inevitable. One can even say that it is precisely in the way life regards death and deals with it in its concern that life displays its way of being. If it flees from the death that stands before it as something inevitable, and wants to conceal and forget it in its concern with the world of relations, this is the flight of life itself in the face of itself – which means precisely that the ultimate possibility-of-being of life becomes an impossibility-of-being. On such a basis, to grasp *Dasein* in its primordial way of being is ultimately impossible. Because the way in which *Dasein* is concerned with death – from which it would like to flee but cannot – informs its very way of being, one must rather emphasize that it is just there, where life voluntarily opens itself to certain death, that it is truly manifest to itself (*JH* 107–8).

It is an intriguing quirk of textual history that this account of Tanabe's was for sixty-five years the sole source for Heidegger's first words on the topic of death. It was only with the appearance in 1989 of the German text of the 'Aristotle Introduction' from October 1922 that his first written thoughts on death reached print.[19] Judging from what has been published so far, there is no evidence that Heidegger had engaged the ideas of death and nothingness on an existential or ontological level before the 'Aristotle Introduction'. And while the lectures from the summer semester of 1923 make cursory reference to such themes as *das Man* and *Angst*, there is no discussion of death or nothingness.[20] The next public presentation of Heidegger's ideas about death (after the winter course of 1923) would appear to be in his lecture 'The Concept of Time', which was delivered in July 1924 in Marburg.[21]

It is interesting to compare Tanabe's account of the 1923 lecture course with the relevant passages in the earlier 'Aristotle Introduction':

> Just as factical life ... is not a process [*Vorgang*], so too death is not a termination of the kind that intrudes and cuts this process short. Death is something that stands in front of [*bevor steht*] factical life as something inevitable. ... The forced lack of worry that characterizes life's concern [*Sorge*] with its death culminates in a fleeing into 'real-worldly' concerns [*Besorgnisse*]. But this looking-away from death is so little a grasping of life in itself that it becomes precisely life's own evasion of life and its authentic being-character. ... In the having of *certain* death (a having that *takes hold*), life becomes visible in itself.[22]

The content (and even the style) of Tanabe's account is quite similar. What appears to distinguish this later version is the talk of life's 'voluntarily [opening] itself to certain death', which anticipates Heidegger's later talk of openness with respect to death but is also characteristic of the Japanese *bushidō*, the 'way of the samurai warrior', a mode of existence influenced by Buddhism and which is also 'the way of death'.

It is clear that Heidegger, when he made Tanabe's acquaintance, was already working towards the existential conception of death that would play such an important role in *Being and Time*; but it is possible that his encounter with this incisive and passionate thinker from the East Asian tradition stimulated him to develop his thinking about death along somewhat different lines from those he might otherwise have followed. Several circumstances tend to strengthen this supposition, the first of which requires a look forward in order to take a step back.

A consideration of the sources Heidegger cites in connection with the full-fledged treatment of the topic of death in *Being and Time* – Dilthey, Simmel, Jaspers (SZ 249, note 1) – reveals a number of familiar elements but nothing like the complex configuration of death and nothingness that so powerfully motivates the existential analysis of authentic temporality in that work. Heidegger lays special emphasis on the relevance of Jaspers' conception of death as a *Grenzsituation* ('limit-situation'), a topic he had discussed earlier in an essay from 1921 on Jaspers' ground-breaking work

Psychologie der Weltanschauungen, first published in 1919.[23] In a discussion of Jaspers' engagement with the problem of comprehending life in its totality, Heidegger quotes and paraphrases as follows:

> 'The relation of the human being to its own death is different from that to all other transitoriness, only the nonbeing of the world as a whole is a comparable idea'. 'Only the destruction of one's own being or of the world as a whole is something *total* for the human being'. There is an 'experiential relation to death', which is not to be confused with a 'general knowing about death', only 'when death has entered into experience [*in das Erleben . . . getreten ist*] as a limit-situation', that is to say, 'only where 'consciousness of the limit and infinitude' has not been lost.[24]

Heidegger refrains from discussing these passages from Jaspers, but the concern with totality, an experiential relation to death, and the idea of death's 'entering into' experience figure importantly in the existential conception of death that he would later elaborate in *Being and Time*. And indeed these passages are from the section of Jaspers' book to which Heidegger draws special attention in the footnote at *Sein und Zeit* 249.[25]

Heidegger's citations in the 'Anmerkungen' break off on page 262 of the third edition of *Psychologie der Weltanschauungen*; on the next page Jaspers begins a discussion of the Buddhist attitude towards death, referring to Buddhism as 'the classic example of *the experience of transitoriness as the central experience* influencing the whole attitude towards life [*Lebensgesinnung*]' (263). Quoting from the Indian Ashvagosha, Jaspers gives an account of the Buddhist attitude towards death as thoroughly nihilistic and pessimistic – an account apparently influenced by the (rather unreliable) interpretations given by Schopenhauer and Nietzsche. The Buddhists are said to renounce the world on account of its transitory nature: 'Death is overcome in so far as everything that can die is experienced as an object of indifference' (264–5). Their desire is for 'the ultimate death' that is found in release from the cycle of death and rebirth: 'Death and transitoriness give rise in the Buddhists to a drive for the eternal reign of the peace of nothingness' (265). While this attitude may be characteristic of certain schools of early (Hinayana) Buddhism, it is the antithesis – as we shall see – of the attitude towards death of later, Mahayana Buddhism.

Tanabe gives another retrospective account (in the late 1950s) of his enthusiastic discovery of Heidegger's ideas about death, in his contribution to the *Festschrift* for the latter's seventieth birthday.[26] He begins by contrasting the general inclination towards philosophies of life in the Western tradition with the more 'death-oriented' approach characteristic of East Asian philosophies. For philosophers in the Buddhist tradition, 'in thinking of the enigmatic inevitability of death, the ephemerality and fragility of life pervade us to the very marrow' ('Todesdialektik', 93–4).

For this reason, Tanabe continues, he had always been dissatisfied in his studies of Western philosophy – until he went to Freiburg. He goes on to recall how deeply impressed he was to discover, on first attending Heidegger's lectures, 'that in his thinking a meditation on death had become central to philosophy and supported it from the ground up. I could not help feeling that I had now found a way to the philosophy I had been seeking'.

This talk of 'meditation on death' as central to Heidegger's thought should not be taken to imply either that Heidegger had by this time developed a full 'philosophy of death' or that Tanabe had been himself innocent of the topic. Since Tanabe's scholarly output prior to his trip to Germany had been largely in the fields of science and mathematics, the encounter with Heidegger appears to have helped him to connect his academic endeavours with a deeper level of his existence. This deeper level had to do with Tanabe's lifelong concern with the philosophy of religion: Christianity had interested him intensely during his school days, and he devoted most of his later career to religious philosophy, undertaking numerous comparisons between Christianity and Japanese Buddhism. It is reasonable to suppose that, at the time he met Heidegger, 'the philosophy [Tanabe] had been seeking' already comprised the problem of death, and that the discovery that Heidegger was working a number of existential concerns into his 'phenomenology of life' showed him that such topics could be engaged philosophically as well as on a personal level.[27]

Otto Pöggeler has shown the relevance of Heidegger's early engagement with Augustine, Luther, and Kierkegaard for the existential analytic he was to develop in *Being and Time*, and their ideas were no doubt an influence on his conceptions of anxiety, death, and nothingness.[28] John Van Buren has provided more details in an informative essay on Heidegger's early engagement with 'primal Christianity'.[29] There is also a striking prefiguration of Heidegger's idea of *Vorlaufen in den Tod* (*SZ*, § 53) in Augustine, who characterizes 'the time of this life' as a 'running to death' (*cursus ad mortem*; *Lauf in den Tod*), a phrase reiterated by Luther.[30] Heidegger is spectacularly grudging in his cursory acknowledgement of Kierkegaard for having developed the concept of anxiety.[31] In view of Tanabe's early interest in the religion, Heidegger's prolonged concern with the 'factical experience of life' in Christianity not long before the former's arrival would make it all the more likely that the two thinkers would spark one another's philosophical interest in the topic of death.[32] Moreover, since Heidegger had written on Jaspers' idea of death as a *Grenzsituation*, and read his discussion of the Buddhist attitude towards death, it is probable that this topic came up in his conversations with Tanabe. And if it did, Tanabe would have explained to him that the attitude towards death of the later (Mahayana) schools of Buddhism is, by contrast with that of early Buddhism, positive and life-promoting – just as their understanding of nothingness is by no means nihilistic.

It was not until two decades later that Tanabe eventually elaborated in detail the 'philosophy of death' that his encounter with Heidegger's ideas had inspired him to develop, in the work that many regard as his master-piece: *Philosophy as Metanoetics* (1946).[33] In the course of frequent dis-cussions of Heidegger, Tanabe criticizes his conceptions of death and nothingness as being insufficiently radical. He implies an elitist quality to Heidegger's account of the way an appropriate confrontation with death leads to authentic existence, suggesting that the resolute facing of death is a way open only to 'sages and heroes' (85). Heidegger's conception is of 'a death interpreted entirely from the standpoint of life, a nothingness interpreted from the standpoint of being'. In laying out his 'positive' ideas about 'living as one who is dead', Tanabe allows that 'Heidegger's position is somewhat similar to Zen imperatives' such as 'Die to yourself once and for all!' and 'Above all else, the Great Death!' (161–2). Tanabe's own posi-tion, based on the notion of 'Other-power' (*tariki*) developed in Shin Buddhism and thus attainable by 'ordinary ignorant people', may be summed up as a 'dialectic of death and life' in which 'just as death does not follow life but is already within life itself, so is life restored within death and mediated by it' (164). This is not the place to present and evaluate Tanabe's position on death, which takes much of the book to be articulated: suffice it to say that the critique of Heidegger deserves to be taken seri-ously, and that Tanabe's engagement with the problem of death here and in other works shows that the issue increases in importance as his thinking matures, while in Heidegger's thought it tends to diminish.

Tanabe continued to develop in print his ideas on 'the enigmatic inevitability of death, the ephemerality and fragility of life' in a work en-titled *Existenz, Love, and Praxis* (1947) in which he proposes that philosophy return to the Socratic conception of the discipline as 'practice for death'. He goes on to link this conception with similar understand-ings from the Christian tradition as well as with the samurai idea of 'the way of death'.[34] An even closer accommodation between Buddhism and Christianity on the topic of death is attempted in the later essay 'Memento Mori' (1958), where the notion of life-death (*shōji ichinyo*) – a perpetual death-and-resurrection *within* every moment of life – becomes the crux.[35] One of Tanabe's formulations of this idea is remarkably similar to a locution Heidegger uses (borrowing from Rilke) in the essay 'What Are Poets For?' In tackling the question of how death can be incorpo-rated into life without leading to nihilism and suicide, Tanabe writes:

> The reason we have been driven to life's self-contradiction is that we have unreflectingly pursued life's direct enjoyment, and as a result have lost the self-perception that life is always 'backed' by death and that we do not know when these two sides will be reversed, with death appearing in front and life driven to the rear. It is a result of going against the injunction 'Forget not death' and of forgetting death.[36]

One final consideration that is relevant here is the fact, generally unknown to Heidegger scholars in the West, that Tanabe's contribution to the 1959 *Festschrift* for Heidegger was a translation of only the second part of the monograph that had been published the previous year, entitled 'Sei no sonzaigaku ka shi no benshōhō ka' (Ontology of life or dialectics of death?) – the original version of which bore the somewhat spirited subtitle 'A polemical engagement with Heideggerian ontology'.[37] Ōhashi Ryōsuke has pointed out that the first half of the monograph, which tact dictated should not be translated for the *Festschrift*, contains some sharp criticism of Heidegger's 'ontology of life'.[38] Tanabe's argument is too long and complex to be rehearsed here, but the gist of his 'polemical engagement' is a continuation of his customary criticisms of Western philosophies as overly oriented towards life and insufficiently mindful of death. Heidegger's understanding of death, he argues, is not radical enough and fails to reach as deeply as his (Tanabe's) own 'dialectics of death' which is based on a late Buddhist understanding of the interfusion of life and death and is elaborated this time by way of a quasi-Hegelian dialectic.

'NISHIDA PHILOSOPHY' AND THE *TOPOS* OF NOTHINGNESS

For several years prior to his visit to Freiburg Tanabe had been a junior colleague of Nishida Kitarō's at Kyoto University. While Nishida was well acquainted with German thought – the mystical tradition, German Idealism, and neo-Kantianism in particular – the philosophy he had begun to elaborate in his masterwork of 1911 was experientially based on the practice of Zen Buddhism and came more and more to turn on the Buddhist conception of nothingness (*mu*).[39] Tanabe would also make the idea of *zettai mu* (absolute nothingness) central to the philosophy of religion he develops in his mature thought – even though his different understanding of the idea became a major point of contention in his subsequent philosophical disagreements with Nishida.[40]

At the conclusion of a chapter of *An Inquiry into the Good* entitled 'The Phenomena of Consciousness as the Sole Reality' (Chapter 6), Nishida suggests that – by contrast with situations in the physical world under the law of causality – in consciousness something *can* arise out of nothing. In a chapter dealing with his conception of God as the ground of reality, he follows the *via negativa* of Nicholas of Cusa and the idea of God as total negation: 'From this standpoint, God is absolute nothingness' (Chapter 7). He goes on to say that 'precisely because He is able to be nothingness, there is no place whatsoever where he is not present, no place where he is not at work'.[41] And in the context of a later invocation of Nicholas of Cusa and Jacob Boehme, Nishida writes:

Nothingness separated from being is not true nothingness; the one separated from the all is not the true one; equality separated from
distinction is not true equality. In the same way that if there is no God
there is no world, if there is no world there is no God.[42]

In the course of the next decade or so, Nishida continued to grapple
with the problem of how, in consciousness, something appears to arise
from nothing, in the context of an ongoing analysis of the nature of
'creative will'. The discussion in *Intuition and Reflection in Self-
Consciousness* (1917), which actually refers more to Western sources (such
as Boehme and Pseudo-Dionysius, Fichte and Bergson) than to East Asian
ones, emphasizes the close connection between creative will and nothingness.

To say that the will comes from, and returns to, creative nothingness
... seems to be in serious contradiction with the law of causality.
However, there is no fact more immediate and indubitable than the
birth of being from non-being, which occurs constantly in the actuality
of our experience. ... When we penetrate to the immediacy of that
creative act which produces being from nothingness, letting no
[logical/scientific] explanations overlay it, we find absolute free will.
... If thought thus creates natural reality, it is itself in turn created by
will, the immediate, absolute process of creation. Beneath these apparently solid cognitive activities, being is constantly being produced by
nothingness.[43]

Later in the same work Nishida speaks again, alluding perhaps to the
Laozi, of a 'birth of being from non-being':

At this level of immediate experience causal thinking has no place;
being is born from nothingness. ...
   Like our will, which is nothingness while it is being, and being while
it is nothingness, this world transcends even the categories of being and
nothingness ... for here being is born from nothingness (157, 166).

Given that Nishida was well read in the Chinese classics and was especially fond of the *Laozi* and *Zhuangzi*, this familiarity would explain his
use of locutions concerning being's being born from nothingness even in
the context of an explication in terms of Western philosophical concepts.[44]
   Nishida further develops his ideas about the self as 'absolute will' in a
work from 1920, *Ishiki no mondai* (*The Problem of Consciousness*), where
he writes that the true self 'exists at the juncture of being and non-being'
and that the world of will 'emerges from nothingness and enters back into
nothingness'.[45] But it is in the essays from the next few years, which were
eventually published in 1927 under the title *Hataraku mono kara miru
mono e* (*From the Acting to the Seeing*), that Nishida elaborates his central
idea of the '*topos* of nothingness' (*mu no basho*) as the *fons et origo* of

all reality. These essays, the earliest of which were written while Tanabe was with Heidegger in Freiburg, unfold the idea of a 'true nothingness' that is not relative to being but is rather a field or 'activity' (the influence of Fichte's idea of *Tathandlung* is evident here) that embraces both being and non-being. The deepest ground of the will is again referred to as a 'creative nothingness' but more often as 'absolute nothingness' (*zettai mu*).[46]

Heidegger scholars assume without question that the revolutionary understanding of nothingness presented in *Being and Time* came out of his creative 'destruction' of the history of Western ontology. Reinhard May has shown the remarkable similarity between the locutions in which Heidegger develops the *topos* of *Nichts* relative to the *topoi* of *Sein* and *Lichtung* in his middle and later periods; but the similarity of the earlier formulations to Nishida's ideas is just as remarkable.[47] While the documentation that would decide the question appears to be lacking, there is one consideration that militates in favour of the possibility that Heidegger learned of, and was influenced by, the idea of nothingness that was being developed by Nishida during the 1920s – and which would come to assume, in the form of 'absolute nothingness', a central place in the philosophy of the Kyoto School.

When Tanabe arrived in Freiburg, Husserl was immediately impressed by his philosophical acumen and was intrigued by what Tanabe had to say about Nishida's philosophy (what is now known in Japan as *Nishida tetsugaku*, 'Nishida philosophy'). According to an account by Aihara Shinsaku, a younger colleague of Tanabe's:

> When Professor Tanabe told him about Nishida's philosophy, Husserl invited him to give some detailed lectures on the topic. Tanabe consequently gave a series of lectures on Nishida's philosophy at Husserl's home ... in the course of which Husserl frequently asked questions. Tanabe's lectures were a great success, and a well known [German] philosopher wrote to Nishida to say that Tanabe's presentations had been outstanding [*ausgezeichnet*].[48]

The audience could not have hoped for a speaker more qualified, since Tanabe had been following closely the development of Nishida's thought for the previous ten years. He was also a fanatically meticulous preparer of lectures and presentations. About the talks he gave at Husserl's home, one of Tanabe's foremost students, Takeuchi Yoshinori, has said: 'If he often stayed up all night composing his lectures just for us students in Kyoto, you can imagine how well prepared he must have been for a presentation in the presence of the great Husserl'. Heidegger was, of course, present at these lectures, though it is not certain that he attended every one of them.[49] The other leading student of Tanabe's, Tsujimura Kōichi, relates how the first session barely got off the ground, thanks to the intervention of a member of the select audience, the mathematician

Ernst Zermelo.[50] Zermelo was apparently so impressed by Tanabe's exper-
tise in the philosophy of mathematics that he began asking questions on
that topic early in the presentation, and ended up steering the rest of the
evening's discussion in the direction of set theory.

In the absence of a direct record of Tanabe's presentations, one can
only speculate on their content. But since Nishida had been developing
his ideas about *mu* since 1911, and Tanabe was at the time the best interpreter of his mentor's thinking, the presentation could not have helped
dealing with Nishida's conception of nothingness (especially since the idea
of *mu* was soon to become so central to Tanabe's own thinking).

In all of his published writings Heidegger mentions Tanabe Hajime only
once, in the 'Conversation on Language', where he has the Japanese say:

> – J: Professor Tanabe often came back to the question you once
> addressed to him of why we Japanese didn't reflect upon the vener-
> able beginnings of our own thinking instead of greedily chasing after
> the latest things in European philosophy.[51]

The 'venerable beginnings' of Japanese thought include philosophical
ideas from classical Daoism and the Zen tradition, as Heidegger well knew
when he composed the dialogue. (More on this in the next section.) He
may also have known by this time that, even though the Kyoto School
thinkers read and wrote a great deal about Hegel, Kierkegaard, Nietzsche,
and his own work, most of them then reverted to a study of their philosophical roots in the East Asian tradition.

* * *

The extent to which influences from Nishida's philosophy may have helped
nourish the development of Heidegger's conception of nothingness is difficult to determine, not only because of lack of conclusive
evidence but also because the conception of nothingness developed by
the Kyoto School thinkers has some of its roots in the Western tradition.
Relevant prefigurations would be the ideas of *das Nichts* found in such
thinkers as Meister Eckhart, Nicholas of Cusa, and Jacob Boehme, with
whom Heidegger was as familiar as Nishida was at the time, as well as in
the idealism of Hegel and Schelling. What makes this topic in the comparative history of ideas even more complicated, as well as more interesting,
is that a strain of Asian thinking about nothingness feeds into the Western
tradition, and into German philosophy in particular, from the end of the
eighteenth century. Near the end of 'What Is Metaphysics?', Heidegger
quotes with approval, though not without qualification, Hegel's well-
known formulation in Book I of the *Science of Logic*: 'Pure Being and
pure Nothing are the same'. It is significant in the present context that
Hegel follows this equation with a pointed reference to Buddhist thought
that Heidegger could not have overlooked: 'In oriental systems, and

especially in Buddhism, *nothingness*, or the void [*das Leere*], is the absolute principle'.[52] We find another reference to Asian ideas of nothingness in Schelling, on whom Heidegger began to give seminars in 1928 (with Kuki Shūzō auditing the first). In *The Philosophy of Mythology* Schelling writes of Laozi's notion of nothingness as follows:

> The great art or wisdom of life consists precisely in attaining this pure potential, which is nothing and yet at the same time all. The entire *Dao de jing* is concerned with showing, through a great variety of the most pregnant tropes, the great and insuperable power of non-being.[53]

A more immediate (though generally unremarked) precursor with respect to a radical notion of nothingness is Max Scheler, whom Heidegger refers to often in his lectures from the 1920s, as well as in *Being and Time*. In his essay 'Vom Wesen der Philosophie' of 1917, Scheler proposed as the fundamental basis of philosophical activity the insight 'that *there is anything at all* or, put more precisely, that "*there is not nothing*" (whereby the word "nothing" ... means *absolute nothing* ...)'.[54] After a discussion of how the circumstance that 'there isn't nothing' prompts philosophical wonderment, Scheler goes on to say: 'Whoever has not looked into the *abyss of absolute nothing* in this way will also completely overlook the eminently positive nature of the content of the insight that there is anything at all and not rather nothing'. This phrasing will be familiar to those acquainted with Heidegger's writings on the topic from the late 1920s and mid-1930s.

In a discussion of religious activity in the essay 'Problems of Religion' (1920), Scheler returns to the topic of absolute nothing:

> To believe in 'nothing' is something quite different from not believing. It is – as evidenced by the powerful emotional impact that the thought of 'nothing' exercises on our soul – a highly positive state of the spirit. *Absolute nothing* is to be sharply distinguished from every merely relative nothing as a phenomenon. Absolute nothing is not-being-something and not-existing in one, in utter unity and simplicity.[55]

In a footnote at this point Scheler says that this unity distinguishes absolute nothing from the Buddhist idea of nirvana, which he (mis-) understands as 'merely freedom and redemption from the actual world'. Although Scheler's enterprise is more explicitly religious than Heidegger's, his talk later in the same paragraph of 'metaphysical *Angst*' and 'religious *Schauder* in the face of absolute nothing' is a striking anticipation of Heidegger's formulations several years later. And again, as with the case of Jaspers mentioned earlier, if the topic of nirvana (as discussed by Scheler) came up in Heidegger's conversations with Tanabe (or, later, with Kuki), any misconceptions of nirvana or nothingness as negative or world-denying would surely have been corrected.

Otto Pöggeler reports Heidegger's saying to him that the Japanese had, much to his surprise, introduced something into the discussion of *das Nichts* that had not previously occurred to him – a most interesting remark, even though it is unclear at what point on his path of thinking this introduction may have occurred.[56] The crucial question here is at what point Heidegger read Ōhazama and Faust's *Zen: Der lebendige Buddhismus in Japan* (1925).[57] Since August Faust had studied with Heidegger in Freiburg in 1922, the latter may well have read this anthology of Zen texts with extensive annotation and commentary shortly after its publication in 1925 – and thus before he wrote *Sein und Zeit*.[58] The question bears directly on the foregoing discussion of nothingness, since Ōhazama's introduction, which includes a comprehensive overview of the development of Mahayana Buddhism, makes it perfectly clear that the Buddhist conceptions of nirvana and nothingness are by no means nihilistic or world-denying. (He gives accounts of such key figures as Nāgārjuna, Rinzai, Dōgen, Bashō, and Hakuin.) The idea of 'perfect' or 'consummate' nothing (*muichimotsu, vollendetes Nichts*) comes up again and again in the Zen texts translated in this volume – as when the Zen master Hakuin writes of one who has seen into his own nature: 'Then his own being is nothing other / than the nature of consummate nothingness, / and is sublimely elevated over the play of thinking'.[59] Ōhazama offers numerous explanations of this consummate nothingness, and Heidegger will also have been intrigued by his explication of the 'twenty-fold' nothingness in the *Prajñāpāramitā Sūtra*.[60]

One last event concerning Heidegger's relationship to Japan during this period should be mentioned, an incident that could have changed the course of Heidegger's thinking prior to the writing of *Being and Time*. In a letter to Karl Jaspers from June 1924, Heidegger writes that he has received an official offer from Japan through a Japanese colleague (Miki Kiyoshi – though Heidegger refrains from naming him for some reason).[61] The offer was for a three-year position at an institute in Tokyo for the study of European culture. Heidegger would have had to give only one lecture or seminar per week, and also collaborate on a quarterly publication of the institute. The financial remuneration would have been handsome, with travel paid for the whole family. 'The advantages would be: broadening of my horizon, the opportunity for undisturbed work, money to build a house after returning. Nevertheless, I am not sure that I need such an excursion or should take on such a thing.'[62]

Heidegger ends by asking Jaspers' advice on whether or not he should accept the offer, and also whether, if not, he should put forward Jaspers' name instead. Unfortunately, Jaspers' reply has not survived. In any case, the possibility that *Being and Time* might have been written in Tokyo surely boggles the mind.

KUKI SHÛZÔ AND LIGHT FROM EAST ASIA

Kuki had been one of the participants with Miki Kiyoshi in Rickert's seminar in Heidelberg in 1923, after which he spent three years in Paris studying French philosophy. He returned to Germany in the spring of 1927 in order to work with Husserl in Freiburg.[63] After meeting Heidegger at Husserl's home, however, Kuki was sufficiently impressed by the younger philosopher that he followed him to Marburg later that year in order to continue sitting in on his classes.[64] Apparently, Kuki was already acquainted with Heidegger's philosophy, since it is mentioned in the first draft of his manuscript on the idea of *iki*, which he had completed in Paris the previous year.[65] His *Haideggā no tetsugaku* (*The Philosophy of Heidegger*) from 1933 would be the first book-length study of Heidegger's thought to be published in any language.

Among the Japanese thinkers who visited Heidegger in the 1920s it was Kuki who seems to have made the most forceful impression.[66] Reinhard May's discussion has pointed out that the major role played by Kuki and his ideas in Heidegger's 'Conversation' on language is quite disproportional to their part in the actual conversation on which the text was based. Nevertheless, the Inquirer's opening statement − 'To Count Kuki belongs my enduring remembrance' − sounds like a genuine expression of the author's feelings. It also rings true, in view of Kuki's reputed charisma, when the Inquirer remarks that the conversations 'unfolded freely and spontaneously [*wie ein freies Spiel*] in our home, where Count Kuki sometimes came with his wife, who would wear traditional Japanese dress' − and that 'the East Asian world would thereby shine more radiantly' (*WL* 4/*US* 89). In view of the major element of free invention in Heidegger's 'Conversation', an attempt to reconstruct the content of the original conversations might do well to proceed from Kuki's side.[67]

Heidegger's Inquirer says that the conversations concerned Kuki's notion of *iki* and, more broadly, 'the essential nature of *East Asian* art and poetry'. Kuki had, in fact, completed a first draft of his seminal work on *iki* in Paris the year before coming to Freiburg, under the title 'Iki no honhitsu' ('The Essence of *iki*'). What is surprising about this treatment, written the year before *Being and Time* was published, is that its methodology clearly derives from Heidegger's hermeneutics. (A note in the first chapter of the final [1930] version refers the reader to Heidegger's discussion of the phenomenology of *Dasein* as 'hermeneutic' at *SZ* 37f.) Ōhashi Ryōsuke has resolved the puzzle by pointing out that a note in the Paris manuscript refers to Tanabe's essay of 1924 (mentioned above) 'A New Turn in Phenomenology'.[68] One can imagine that Heidegger's puzzlement over the notion of *iki* would have been tempered by the pleasant surprise that the author of a treatise on it had already adopted the hermeneutical method outlined in *Being and Time*, which had only just been published.

In *The Structure of 'iki'* Kuki distinguishes three 'moments' in the notion of *iki*, which he sees as being distinctive of East Asian cultures, and of Japanese culture in particular.[69] He goes on to suggest, however, that the French '*coquetterie*', supplemented by connotations of 'chic', 'elegance', and 'refinement', comes close to capturing the first of the three moments (*IK* 11–12). This coquetry has to do with a sexual attraction between a man and a woman that is cultivated without being consummated, and is defined as 'a dualistic attitude in which the unitary self posits the other sex opposite itself, constituting a possible relationship between itself and the other sex' (*IK* 17). Since the paradigm for this first moment is to be found in the relationship between the geisha and her patron in the 'gay quarter' of Yoshiwara in eighteenth-century Tokyo, it is not surprising that one finds no mention of this central aspect of *iki* in Heidegger's 'Conversation'. Indeed it would be hard to imagine an atmosphere more remote from Heidegger's milieu than the 'floating world' of Edo-period Japan. The only feature of this moment that might have appealed to him is Kuki's emphasis on coquetry as embodying the *possibility* of sexual union and his insistence that the phenomenon is destroyed if the possibility is allowed to become an actuality.[70]

The other two moments of *iki*, into which coquetry can be, as it were, sublimated, are the ideal of *bushidō*, the 'way of the samurai warrior', and the 'resignation' (*akirame*) of Buddhism. Kuki writes: 'Within *iki* the ideal of bushido is still very much alive' (IK 19); and while he elucidates this ideal as a sublimation of the first moment with reference to the resolute pride of the geisha, it is important for our purposes to note that the major maxim of bushido is: 'The way of the samurai is the way of death'. While the basic idea here is the warrior's willingness to sacrifice his life for his lord, the more existential aspect of it is exemplified in the way the attitude of the warrior on entering combat is generalized to the rest of his behaviour: only by totally extirpating the drive for self-preservation, by fully embracing his death in advance, will the warrior be capable of fighting at the top of his form.[71]

Although this aspect of *iki* also goes unmentioned in Heidegger's 'Conversation', another consideration makes it more likely that the bushido ideal was a topic of his actual conversations with Kuki. After his time in Marburg, Kuki went back to France, and in August 1928 he delivered two lectures in French at a colloquium at Pontigny under the title 'Propos sur le temps'.[72] Since these lectures must have been prepared while Kuki was in Marburg, it is likely that he discussed them with Heidegger – especially since the second talk, entitled 'The Expression of the Infinite in Japanese Art', deals precisely with what Heidegger's 'Inquirer' would later refer to as 'the essential nature of *East Asian* art and poetry'. In the first talk, 'The Notion of Time and Repetition in Oriental Time', Kuki deals mainly with Hindu and Buddhist ideas of temporality, but he also discusses bushido. The talk begins with a reference to Heidegger's contention in *Being and Time* that '"the primordial phenomenon" of time is the future ... the *Sich-vorweg-sein* (being-ahead-of-itself)'.[73] It is possible that Heidegger was already acquainted with bushido, perhaps from conversations with Tanabe, but assuming that 'the way of death' came up in his conversations with Kuki, there must have been astonishment on both sides at the parallels with the existential conception of death in *Being and Time*. This characterization of the idea of 'running forward' to engage one's death, in particular, reads like a passage from a Zen swordsmanship manual:

> When *Dasein* by running forward to its death lets death assume power over it, it understands itself, free for death, in the superior power of its own finite freedom in order to ... become clear-sighted for whatever might befall in the situation thus revealed. ... Only a being that is essentially *futural* in its being, such that, free for its death and shattering itself [*zerschellend*] against it, it can let itself be thrown back on to its actual situation ... can be *momentary* [augenblicklich] for 'its time'.[74]

One of the earlier sources in Europe for an understanding of bushido was the work of Kuki's mentor Okakura Kakuzō, who introduced many of the underlying principles of Japanese culture to the West with the publication in English of *The Ideals of the East with Special Reference to the Art of Japan* in 1903. Kuki's second set of *propos* opens with a reference to Okakura, and he could hardly have talked with Heidegger about Japanese art without recommending his mentor's work.[75] Heidegger certainly came across Okakura's name later, when he read *Zen: Der lebendige Buddhismus in Japan*, in the preface to which the editor recommends Okakura's *Die Ideale des Ostens* (Leipzig 1923) as 'a beautiful introduction to the history of Japanese culture' (p. xi).

Heinrich Petzet also cites Okakura in the context of a discussion of Heidegger's acquaintance with Asian thought. Apparently, Heidegger came to be very interested in Chinese and Japanese art, and when Petzet had to write a review of an exhibition of Zen paintings and drawings, Heidegger 'brought [his] attention to the literature on the subject that seemed to him important'.[76] Assuming that works by Okakura were among the literature Heidegger thought important, he will have learned from them much about Daoism and the Zen-inspired arts of Japan, such as Noh drama and *tanka* and *haiku* poetry (with which he was certainly familiar by the time he wrote the dialogue with the Japanese visitor). He would in any case have been introduced to these things by Kuki, since they figure prominently in the text of his talk on Japanese art.[77]

To return to the idea of *iki*: the third moment, briefly, has to do with Buddhist resignation. Kuki writes that the 'background' of *iki* comprises two aspects:

the Buddhist worldview, which regards the ephemeral and imperma-
nent as the realm of distinctions and emptiness and nirvana as that of
assimilations, and also the religious view that preaches resignation in
the face of evil and detached contemplation of fate (*IK* 21).

This idea of Kuki's may be the pretext for Heidegger's introduction of
the idea of *Leere* (emptiness) into the 'Conversation' – though in connection with Noh drama, an art form far removed from the milieu of the
Edo period exemplified by *iki*. If we recall that Tezuka, in his account of
his hour with Heidegger, mentions Kuki only at the beginning and briefly,
and says nothing whatsoever about the idea of *iki*, it seems likely that the
'Conversation' is indeed 'a kind of confession' in which Heidegger finally
acknowledges his acquaintance with Japanese ideas to which Kuki had
introduced him almost thirty years earlier.[78] If *iki* was not a topic of his
conversation with Tezuka, since no German translation of Kuki's work
was available, Heidegger would have had to cast his mind back quite some
way in order to remember what Kuki had said about it – which no doubt
explains why the explication of *iki* in the 'Conversation' bears so little
relation to Kuki's own presentation of the idea.

Since Reinhard May has discussed this text in detail, as a simultaneous
revelation and concealment of the East Asian influences on Heidegger's
thought, it will suffice to adduce one further consideration in favour of
regarding it as a kind of confession. At one point the Inquirer says to the
Japanese that his visit is especially welcome since his experience in translating German literature (including Heidegger's essays on Hölderlin) into
Japanese will have given him (the Japanese) 'a keener ear for *the questions that I addressed to your compatriots almost thirty-five years ago*' (*WL*
8/*US* 94; emphasis added). The Inquirer then adds in his next speech the
understatement: 'and yet I think that in the meantime I have learned a
thing or two [*einiges*] to help me inquire better than several decades ago'.
Let us simply recall that this dialogue, written thirty years after
Heidegger's contact with Tanabe, Miki, and Kuki in the 1920s, contains
the *only* references to Japanese ideas in Heidegger's works published in
the West so far.

In the second of his talks for the Pontigny colloquium, Kuki quotes
from no fewer than nine chapters of the *Dao de jing* (Laozi) and also
refers to the other major classic of philosophical Daoism, the *Zhuangzi*;
and at the conclusion of another talk given around the same time he
mentions Zen, the Buddhist idea of nothingness, the polarity of *yin* and
yang in the *I jing*, and the philosophy of Nishida (*KS* 72, 97). As Reinhard
May has observed, (near complete) German translations of the Daoist
classics had been available since 1870.[79] Heidegger was surely familiar
with these texts even before his conversations with Kuki; but even if it
were Kuki who first introduced him to Daoist ideas, Heidegger would
have had to go no farther than the university library or bookshop in
Marburg to find German editions of the relevant texts.

Another factor making the milieu of Marburg more conducive to research into things East Asian was the presence on the faculty there, when Heidegger joined it in 1923, of Rudolf Otto, a scholar famous for his research on mysticism and the idea of the numinous. Heidegger had long been interested in the texts of Meister Eckhart, and so he no doubt read an article Otto published in 1925 comparing Eckhart's ideas with Eastern mysticism.[80] This topic would receive an extended discussion in Otto's *Mysticism East and West*, the first German edition of which was published the following year. Also in 1925, Otto wrote a foreword to Ōhazama and Faust's anthology, in which he speaks of Zen as the basis for the samurai code of bushido (pp. iv–v). He begins the foreword with a reference to his own earlier discussion of Zen based on texts published in *The Eastern Buddhist* (p. iii), a venerable journal founded in Kyoto shortly after the turn of the century. In that earlier essay Otto reports that Japanese philosophers consider Eckhart (as they do to this day) to be the Western thinker who comes closest to Zen.[81]

In his editor's preface August Faust makes a highly significant remark (p. xii) in the course of describing the preparations he and Ōhazama engaged in before embarking on the extremely difficult work of translating Zen texts into a Western language. He reports that they read some texts in Western philosophy together, including at least one by Heinrich Rickert, and that some of the philosophical terminology employed in their translation was derived from Emil Lask. Rickert had been Heidegger's teacher at Freiburg (until 1916), and was the dedicatee of his *Habilitationsschrift*, while Heidegger acknowledges Lask's work as the most important influence on him at that time.[82] A bizarre coincidence – that such alien texts as the classics of Chinese and Japanese Zen should become accessible to Heidegger through the linguistic idiom of his philosophical mentors!

By 1927, then, Heidegger had engaged in philosophical dialogue with three of the greatest thinkers of twentieth-century Japan, whose formidable intellects covered a range of fields: philosophy of science and religion (Tanabe), social and political thought (Miki), and metaphysics and aesthetics (Kuki). He had been introduced to the philosophy of Nishida, and had had ample opportunity to learn about the Buddhist idea of nothingness, the affinity between Meister Eckhart and Zen, and the basic ideas of Daoist thought.

SIGNS FROM THE 'MIDDLE PERIOD'

The story of Heidegger's relations with Japanese philosophers after his contact with Kuki Shūzō in 1927–8 can be recounted fairly briefly. The year 1930 is important, not only because Heidegger is definitely known to have been familiar with Buber's *Zhuangzi* by that time, but also because the first translation of Heidegger's work into Japanese was made that year.

(Another 'first' for the Japanese.) The Japanese edition of 'What Is Metaphysics?', which appeared a year after the original had been published, was translated by Yuasa Seinosuke, who had come to Germany in 1926 and stayed until the late 1930s. After studying with Karl Jaspers for a year in Heidelberg, Yuasa went to Freiburg in 1929 to study with Heidegger. In view of Reinhard May's discussion in Chapter 3 above, and of the manifold opportunities Heidegger had had by this time to learn about East Asian conceptions of nothingness from his Japanese colleagues, it is hardly surprising that the translation of 'What Is Metaphysics?' was – as Heidegger himself would later put it – 'understood immediately' by its Japanese readers.[83] The philosopher to whom Heidegger wrote these words, Kojima Takehiko, had studied with Nishida and Tanabe in Kyoto, and had visited Heidegger at his home in Messkirch in 1955.[84]

The news of a Japanese translation of his work and its enthusiastic acceptance in a country as culturally distant as Japan is likely to have encouraged Heidegger's interest in East Asian ideas. The highly poetic form of the Daoist and Zen classics appears to have impressed Heidegger as much as their content. Even though, to borrow an image from a Ming dynasty writer (quoted by Okakura), a translation is like the reverse side of a brocade – all the threads are there, but without the subtlety of the colours or the design – these texts (the *Laozi* and *Zhuangzi* especially) are so poetic that much of their beauty can come across in translation. And indeed Heidegger's encounter with them appears to have contributed to a twofold effect on his thinking: for one thing his prose begins to change from the uncompromisingly functional language of *Being and Time* to the more poetic evocations of 'On the Essence of Truth' (1930), and for another, he begins to develop one of the major themes of his mature thinking – concerning the closeness of philosophical thought and poetry.[85]

In his lectures on metaphysics from the summer of 1935, Heidegger remarks that the only thing that is of the same order as philosophy and its thinking is *Dichtung*. Although they are not the same, he continues, the only people other than philosophers who are able to talk about *das Nichts* are poets. In a pronouncement that could have issued from the pen of a commentator on the thinker-poet Bashō (in whose work Heidegger developed a keen interest), he writes: 'In the poetizing of the poet and the thinking of the thinker, there is always so much world-space bestowed that in it any thing whatsoever – a tree, a mountain, a house, a bird-call – completely loses its indifference and ordinariness'.[86]

Heidegger's *An Introduction to Metaphysics* contains what may be the first published references to the Japanese, but they appear simply in lists of examples of what there is (*Seiendes*). But when it comes to a discussion of philosophies that have 'inquired about the ground of the things that are', no mention is made of the East Asian traditions with which Heidegger was by that time quite familiar: only thinkers who think in the medium of Greek or German, 'the most powerful and spiritual language[s] with regard to the possibility of thinking',[87] are deemed capable of inquiring into that ground.

'The Origin of the Work of Art' from the following year (1936) constitutes Heidegger's first and longest meditation on the topic of art and betokens a further shift in the direction of his thinking. The original stimulus for his engagement with this topic may well have been his conversations about art with Kuki in 1927 and 1928; this essay, at any rate, shows the most influence from East Asian thought among the works of the middle period. A shorthand (if rather immodest) way of showing this is to recommend a reading of my 'Thoughts on the Way' – part of which was intended as an excursus on resonances between Heidegger's texts of 1935/6 and Daoist philosophical ideas – as a catalogue of the *influences* of Daoism on Heidegger's thinking of the mid-1930s.[88] On the assumption that Heidegger had read the Richard Wilhelm translation of the *I jing* (published in 1923), one can, for example, see his idea of truth as the *Riss* denoting the interplay of *Welt* and *Erde* as an adaptation of the notion of the *dao* as the common source of the cyclical forces of *qian* and *kun* (which correspond closely to the forces of *yang* and *yin*).[89]

In the light of Heidegger's contact with Nishida's ideas (as mediated by Tanabe and probably also by Kuki), an obscure but central passage in 'The Origin of the Work of Art' becomes clearer. In the course of a discussion of truth as the unconcealment produced by the struggle of world and earth, Heidegger says more about the *Lichtung*, the illuminated clearing that in *Being and Time* had been equated with *Dasein* and which now appears co-extensive with *Sein* itself and *das Nichts*.

> Beings stand in Being [*Das Seiende steht im Sein*]. . . .
> And yet, beyond beings – though not away from them but this side of them – something Other is happening. Amidst beings in totality there is an open space. A clearing is there. From the perspective of beings it is 'beinger' than beings [*seiender als das Seiende*]. The open middle is thus not surrounded by beings, but the central illumining clearing itself encircles – like the Nothing we hardly know – all that is (*PLT* 53/*Hw* 41).

Here, complementary to the Daoist ideas, is something like the Zen Buddhist idea of nothingness: *mu*, or *kū* – emptiness, distinct but not different from form. Heidegger's *Lichtung* may be seen as the German version of Nishida's *mu no basho*, or *topos* of nothingness.[90] Nishida had begun in the mid-1920s to use a striking image to express the way the *topos* of absolute nothingness 'backs' or 'lines' all the other spheres of human activity and thought, in the way the lining of a garment completes it but remains invisible from the outside.[91]

The topic of Heidegger's relations to Nishida is a fascinating one that calls for more research. D. T. Suzuki reports that in a conversation with Heidegger in 1953 he asked him what he thought of Nishida's philosophy;

Heidegger's response was: 'Nishida is Western'.[92] One wonders about the basis for this remarkable comment. Four essays by Nishida had appeared in German by that time, three of them in a rather opaque translation; but this judgement of Heidegger's may also derive from conversations with his Japanese visitors. His near silence concerning Nishida echoes his near silence concerning Tanabe: although Heidegger never had personal contact with the former, Nishida's niece, Takahashi Fumi, studied with Heidegger in the later 1930s, and his son-in-law, Kaneko Takezō, visited him during the 1960s.[93]

To return to 'The Origin of the Work of Art', Heidegger drops an enigmatic allusion to the source of that essay in a *Zusatz* he added in 1956. (The editor of the new edition of *Holzwege*, in which the supplement is included after the *Nachwort*, remarks that 'Heidegger repeatedly emphasized the importance of this 'supplement' in conversation'.)[94] The *Zusatz* is concerned mainly with resolving the apparent opposition between the 'establishing of truth' (in the work of art) and a 'letting the advent of truth occur', and emphasizes that 'this *Lassen* is not any kind of passivity but' – just like *wu wei* in Daoism – 'the highest kind of doing'. The last paragraph contains a striking remark:

> It remains an inevitable difficulty that the reader, who naturally comes upon the essay from the outside, at first and in the long run does not think of and interpret its content from the secret source of what is to be thought [*nicht aus dem verschwiegenen Quellbereich des Zudenkenden*].

One wonders why the source of what is to be thought should be so secret – if only because *Quelle* is the term Heidegger uses soon after in discussing the possible basis for dialogue between Western and East Asian thought.[95]

After this highly productive period from 1935 to 1936, another visitor from Japan arrived, Nishitani Keiji, a student of Nishida's with an intense interest in Nietzsche. Nishitani was to stay in Germany until 1938, attending Heidegger's seminars in Freiburg and having many informal conversations with him at his home.[96] Nishitani relates how in 1938 he presented Heidegger with a copy of the first volume of D. T. Suzuki's *Essays in Zen Buddhism*, only to find that he had already read the book and was eager to discuss it.[97] In conversation in Kyoto in 1989, Professor Nishitani recounted how Heidegger had given him 'a standing invitation' to come to his house on Saturday afternoons to talk about Zen. Heidegger was apparently most interested in the striking imagery that characterizes so many of the classical Zen texts. He would have found excellent examples in the Ōhazama and Faust collection, which translates excerpts from such works as *The Gateless Gate* (*Mumonkan*) and *The Blue Cliff Records* (*Hekiganroku*) that are rife with wild Zen imagery. Nishitani also concurs with other East Asian interlocutors in saying that Heidegger was always an avid and insightful questioner when it came to the topic of Asian thought.[98] In a brief note written on the occasion of Heidegger's death, Nishitani made the following pregnant observation:

> With respect to metaphysics Heidegger wanted to go a step further and inquire into what lies beneath it. It became clear that this attempt made direct contact with Eastern insights, such as those of Laozi, Zhuangzi, and Zen Buddhism. For this reason Heidegger used to question me about Zen Buddhism.[99]

Let me conclude by remarking upon an interesting reaction to some of Heidegger's middle period works on the part of Karl Jaspers, who is an important figure in this story as a long-standing friend of Heidegger's whose admiration for Asian thought was as open as the latter's was concealed. Jaspers was spending the summer of 1949 in the 'Nietzsche country', when he wrote to Heidegger from St Moritz on 6 August to thank him for sending three recently published books: the new edition of *What Is Metaphysics?* with the introduction and afterword, and the second editions of *On the Essence of Truth* and the *Letter on Humanism*.[100] Jaspers writes:

> Many questions arise for me. I have still not managed to get to the mid-point of the whole thing. It helps somewhat to think of Asian ideas, which I've been interested in for years, knowing well that I lack a penetrating understanding, and yet finding myself wonderfully stimulated from that direction. Your 'Being', the 'clearing of Being', your reversal of our relation to Being into Being's relation to us, the remainder of Being itself – I seem to have perceived something of the sort in Asia. That you are driving toward that at all, and – according to your interpretation of *Being and Time* – always have done, is extraordinary.

It is most interesting, in view of Reinhard May's discussion of the *topoi* of Being and the clearing, that Jaspers (whose understanding of Asian thought had certainly become more 'penetrating' since his characterization of Buddhism as 'nihilistic' and 'pessimistic' in 1919), should find Heidegger's discussion of these *topoi* reminiscent of 'something of the sort in Asia'. Nor is it surprising that Heidegger should decline to take up the cue.

> What you say about Asian ideas is exciting [*aufregend*]: a Chinese who attended my lectures on Heraclitus and Parmenides from 1943–44 [Paul Hsiao] also found resonances with Eastern thinking. Where I am unfamiliar with the language I remain sceptical [*skeptisch*]; and I became all the more so when the Chinese, who is himself a Christian theologian and philosopher, translated a few verses of Laotse with me. Through questioning I learned how completely alien that kind of language [*Sprachwesen*] is; we then abandoned the attempt. Nevertheless there is something very exciting here, and in my opinion something

essential for the future. ... The resonances presumably have a quite different root: since 1910 I have been accompanied by the master of learning and life Eckhardt; this and the ever-renewed attempt to think through the *to gar auto noein estin te kai einai* of Parmenides; the constant question of the *auto*, which is neither *noein* nor *einai*; the lack of the subject–object relationship in the Greeks brought me – along with my own thinking – to something that looks like a turn-around [*Umkehrung*] and yet is something different and prior.[101]

It is clear from the second half of the paragraph that what Heidegger finds 'exciting' is the prospect of exploring the nature of Asian languages and ideas, rather than his friend's finding resonances between Heidegger's ideas and Asian thought. (Though one could perhaps stretch the meaning of *aufregend* to take it to suggest that Heidegger finds Jaspers' association of his thinking with Asian ideas *annoying*.)

While Heidegger's point about Meister Eckhart and the Greeks is well taken, there is nevertheless still something disingenuous about his deprecatory account of the translation project with Paul Hsiao and his peremptory dismissal of Jaspers' finding of resonances with Asian ideas. Given his familiarity with Daoism two decades before (at the time of the composition of the first two texts he had sent Jaspers), and that by ten years earlier he had become quite familiar – through the tutelage of Nishitani – with Zen ideas, Heidegger's flat denial of any 'resonances with Eastern thinking' speaks volumes.

Jaspers actually mentions 'Laotse' in his subsequent reply; but since this elicits no further comment he sensibly drops the topic.

AMBIVALENCE OVER EAST–WEST DIALOGUE

Since Heidegger's eventual acknowledgement that he had learned something from his contact with thinkers from Japan took place some thirty years after the fact, Reinhard May has scrutinized the text of that acknowledgement for a kind of confession and found one.[102] In view of the amount of contact Heidegger had with East Asian thinkers, the fact of his acquaintance with philosophical texts from that tradition, and the keen intensity with which he used to question his Japanese and Chinese interlocutors about those texts, the references to East Asian ideas in his published works are indeed remarkably few. As one might expect, under the circumstances, they are informed by a certain amount of ambivalence. As has been pointed out above (Chapter 1, note 7) there are, aside from the 'Conversation' (1959), only three instances, in texts published during the previous two years.

In a discussion of the term *Ereignis* in 'Der Satz der Identität' (1957), Heidegger writes that the word 'can no more be translated than the Greek word *logos* or the Chinese Tao'.[103] At the time, few readers of the essay would have known that Heidegger was speaking from experience – having spent a summer, ten years earlier, working with Paul Hsiao on translating chapters of the *Laozi* containing the word *dao*.[104] In 1958 Heidegger completed the essay 'Das Wesen der Sprache', and Reinhard May has shown how the two paragraphs on *Tao*, 'the key word in the poetic thinking of Laotse' (*WL* 92/*US* 198), shed light on Heidegger's frequent use of the key word *Weg* in his writings before and since. Finally, an essay 'Grundsätze des Denkens', published in a journal the same year – and not included in any subsequent edition of Heidegger's works – cites the line from the *Laozi*: 'Whoever knows his brightness veils himself in his darkness'.[105] If the jaded reader takes this as an ironical comment on Heidegger's attitude towards Light from the East, the less cynical observer will still have to judge his mentions of Daoist and Japanese thought as significant in their grudging paucity.

As if to supplement these scant acknowledgements, Heidegger allows himself the occasional discussion of the possibility of dialogue between the Western and East Asian philosophical traditions. In view of his reticence concerning how much his own thinking has appropriated from East Asian thought, it is no surprise to find him vacillating on the issue of cross-cultural philosophical dialogue.

In the essay 'Science and Reflection' from 1953, Heidegger emphasizes that every meditation on the present situation must be rooted in 'our historical *Dasein*' by way of 'a dialogue with the Greek thinkers and their language' – and laments that such a dialogue has not yet begun.[106] He then adds, almost in passing: '[This dialogue] has hardly even been prepared yet, and remains in turn the precondition for our inevitable dialogue with the East Asian world'. Despite its putative inevitability, the Inquirer in the 'Conversation' expresses doubts as to the very possibility of such a dialogue, on the grounds that if language is the house of Being 'we Europeans presumably inhabit a quite different house from the East Asians' (*WL* 5/*US* 90).

> I do not yet see whether what I am trying to think as the essential nature [*Wesen*] of language is *also* adequate to the nature of East Asian language – whether in the end, which would at the same time be the beginning, thinking experience can be reached by an essence of language that would ensure that Western European and East Asian saying can enter into dialogue in such a way that there sings something that wells up from a single source [*Quelle*] (*WL* 8/*US* 94).

Later in the conversation the Inquirer appears to be more convinced that 'for East Asian and European peoples the essential nature of language (*Sprach*wesen) remains quite different' (*WL* 23/*US* 113). The Japanese visitor, however, seems decidedly more sanguine. In talking about his experience of translating Heidegger's essay on Hölderlin's *Heimkunft* and some poems by Kleist, he says:

In the course of the translating it often seemed as if I were wandering back and forth between two different language-essences, and yet in such a way that every now and then something shone forth that made me think that the essential source [*Wesensquell*] of fundamentally different languages might be the same.[107]

Since 'the Japanese' in this dialogue is at least ninety per cent Heidegger, we can understand this discrepancy as representing genuine ambivalence on the part of the author rather than a burst of objective reportage or a sudden access of ability to write dramatic dialogue.

In the context of a discussion of the possibility of 'planetary thinking' in 'Zur Seinsfrage' (1955), Heidegger remarks that neither side is equal yet to the encounters that the cultivation of planetary thinking will require: 'This holds equally for the European and East Asian languages, and above all for the realm of their possible dialogue. Neither of them can by itself open up and ground this realm' (*QB* 107/*Wm* 252). A hint of how this realm might begin to be opened up is given in a passage quoted earlier from the 1959 essay 'Hölderlins Erde und Himmel', where Heidegger speaks in vatic tones of the 'great beginning' of Western thought.

There can of course be no going back to it. Present as something waiting over against us, the great beginning becomes something small. But nor can this small something remain any longer in its Western isolation. It is opening itself to the few other great beginnings that belong with their Own to the Same of the beginning of the infinite relationship, in which the earth is included.[108]

The opening anticipated here must at the very least be an opening to the 'great beginning' of East Asian thought, wherever one locates it.

There is more talk of beginnings in the open letter of 1963 to Kojima Takehiko, also quoted earlier, where Heidegger writes of the necessity for 'the step back' (*der Schritt zurück*) if human beings are to escape the domination of positivism, as exemplified in the tendency for *das Stellen*, and find the way by which they can come into their own:

The step back does not mean a flight of thinking into bygone ages, and least of all a reanimation of the beginnings of Western philosophy. ...The step back is rather the step out of the track in which the progress and regress of ordering [*Bestellen*] take place (*JH* 224).

Backtracking, a step off the path could well bring us back to one of those 'other great beginnings' mentioned earlier – and would thus be a prime instance of *reculer pour mieux sauter*.

It is in the next paragraph of this letter that Heidegger talks about the immediate comprehension in Japan of his discussion of nothingness in 'What Is Metaphysics?' – which suggests that the step out of the progress-regress opposition (which might be accomplished by our opening up to another great beginning) could take us into the realm of nothingness as emptiness. This surmise is confirmed by a comment at the end of the letter, where he alludes to the possibility of a contemplative reconciliation with

> the still hidden mystery of the power of *Stellen* ... [which] is no longer to be accomplished by Western European philosophy up till now, but also not without it – that is, not unless its newly appropriated tradition is brought on to the appropriate path (*JH* 226).

Again the implication is that the reappropriation of the Western philosophical tradition will require a preliminary move out of it, optimally by way of a tradition innocent of the metaphysical ideas that gave rise to the modern Western worldview.

Confirmation for this surmise would appear to come from a remark Heidegger made two years later in the *Der Spiegel* interview of 1966, where he alludes to the possibility that 'some day there might surface in Russia and in China ancient traditions of a "thinking" that might help make it possible for human beings to have a free relationship to the technical world'.[109] Advocates of philosophical dialogue with East Asian traditions will be disappointed, however, by Heidegger's next move with respect to this issue (a page later), which seems to constitute a less helpful *Schritt zurück*. He is responding to a query about an earlier pronouncement of his concerning the 'question mark placed before the task of the Germans' by Hölderlin and Nietzsche:

> I am convinced that it is only from the same part of the world in which the world of modern technology arose that a reversal can come about, and that it cannot happen by way of an adoption of Zen Buddhism or any other oriental experience of the world. In order to think differently we need the help of the European tradition and a reappropriation of it. Thinking is only transformed by a thinking that is of the same descent and provenance.

As a dismissal of a naive substitution of Eastern wisdom for Western thinking, this passage is clearly unobjectionable. However, the point of a number of Heidegger's earlier and later remarks on this topic seems to be precisely that a proper 'reappropriation' of the European tradition would occur by way of a 'step back out of [that] track' and an opening towards an 'other great beginning' – and that at this point in its history European thinking requires the injection of ideas from an *other* source. A psychologically inclined hermeneutics would want to ask what complex prompted Heidegger to bring up the topic of Zen Buddhism, which he had never mentioned in four decades of published works, only to dismiss its relevance in a tone that smacks of Eurocentric isolationism. This talk of a unilateral reappropriation of the European tradition rings somewhat hollow in view of the preceding pronouncements concerning the *un*feasibility of precisely that – and the desirability of a bilateral approach involving East Asian thought.

This sole mention of Zen Buddhism recalls a reference to it by a German friend of Heidegger's, as recounted in the often dismissed anecdote by William Barrett: 'A German friend of Heidegger told me that one day when he visited Heidegger he found him reading one of Suzuki's books. "If I understand this man correctly", Heidegger remarked, "this is what I have been trying to say in all my writings"'.[110] This book was probably the first volume of Suzuki's *Essays in Zen Buddhism*, which contains several discussions of the Buddhist notion of nothingness as well as numerous references to Meister Eckhart, and which Nishitani in 1938 discovered Heidegger already owned. In any case, Heidegger's remark takes on a new significance in the light of his familiarity with the contents of the Ōhazama and Faust volume.

Suspicions that Heidegger may be speaking differently to a domestic audience and to the Japanese are confirmed by a passage written in 1968, in which he appears to be optimistic again about the possibility of opening up a realm for thinking dialogue between the cultures. In the foreword to the Japanese translation of his lecture 'Zur Frage nach der Bestimmung der Sache des Denkens' he writes:

> By thinking the clearing and characterizing it adequately, we reach a realm that can perhaps make it possible to bring a transformed European thinking into a fruitful engagement with East Asian 'thinking'. Such an engagement could help with the task of saving the essential nature of human being from the threat of an extreme technological reduction and manipulation of human *Dasein*.[111]

Given the importance of that task, and Heidegger's dialogue with Japanese philosophers over a period of forty years, one would like to read the 'doves' feet' (as they are called in German) around the second 'thinking' not as indicative of second-rate thought but as acknowledging a difference between equals.

* * *

In the course of putting together the collection *Heidegger and Asian Thought*, I had the opportunity for a conversation with Professor H.-G. Gadamer. I asked him why, in view of Heidegger's long-term acquaintance with and enthusiasm for Daoist thought (the question and response apply equally well to the case of Zen), there were so few mentions of Daoism in his published texts. He replied that a scholar of Heidegger's generation and calibre would be reluctant to write anything about a philosophy if he were unable to read the relevant texts in the original language. In view of the foregoing exposition, this response may seem disingenuous. (A similar inability certainly did not deter predecessors from Leibniz to

Nietzsche from writing about Asian ideas and saying some interesting things about them.) It is, of course, possible to understand Heidegger's reticence as stemming from an intellectual modesty, from his being unsure whether he really understands these ideas from an alien tradition couched in a language so different from those with which he is familiar. But on the other hand, he did have numerous opportunities – which he apparently seized with alacrity – to question some of the foremost Japanese thinkers of the century precisely about the basic philosophical ideas of the East Asian tradition.

At any rate, the topic calls for further research and close attention to any relevant evidence. In view of the success with which Heidegger's translation work on the *Laozi* was kept secret, however, little of substance is to be expected from his *Nachlass*. While it is possible in the case of Nietzsche, ironically, to determine many of the books he borrowed from the libraries at Schulpforta and the University of Basel, inquiries into Heidegger's borrowing habits at the libraries at Freiburg and Marburg are met with a flat denial ('Keinerlei Unterlagen!') that any pertinent records exist. Corresponding research in Japan is hampered by the fact that so few letters and diaries belonging to the relevant figures have been preserved. In addition, contemporary Japanese scholars seem strangely diffident towards the suggestion that the sympathetic resonances – so often remarked upon there – between Heidegger's thought and ideas from the Japanese tradition may be due in part to bi-directional influence. Perhaps because Heidegger is the highest divinity in the Japanese philosophical pantheon it is difficult to imagine that some of his powers could have derived from the philosophically less prolific indigenous tradition.

Nothing in this essay is intended to deny that Heidegger produced one of the most profound, complex, and influential philosophies of the twentieth century: the question is whether the provenance of that philosophy is as exclusively Graeco-Teutonic as its author would have us believe. Even at this stage of the investigation, the conclusion is unavoidable that Heidegger was less than generous in acknowledging how much he learned from the East Asian tradition.[112] But what is most important here are the implications for how we read Heidegger's texts – especially as more comparative studies are undertaken, but also in the context of the Western tradition *simpliciter*. The possibility that he may have absorbed a considerable amount from an alien philosophical but non-metaphysical tradition prompts, at the very least, the adoption of a different perspective on Heidegger's claims – however justified they may be – to have overcome or subverted the tradition of Western metaphysics.

In the absence of confirmatory texts (letters, transcripts, and so on), scholars with a stake in regarding Heidegger's philosophy as exclusively Western in its genealogy may persist in taking the similarities between his ideas and those of his Japanese colleagues as purely coincidental. Taken on its own, the present essay could then be understood as a study of one of those remarkable coincidences in the history of ideas, where similar patterns of thinking are developed simultaneously by different thinkers in the absence of any influence. But as a complement to the evidence adduced by Reinhard May in the main body of this volume, this essay is a call for a reorientation of our assessment of Heidegger's place in the 'planetary thinking' that is beginning to appear on our horizons as the millennium draws near.

NOTES

1 I am grateful to Professor Michiko Yusa of Western Washington University for providing a number of very helpful comments on the penultimate draft of this essay. Some of the material in what follows appeared earlier, under the more pugnacious title 'Heidegger and Japanese Philosophy: How Much Did He Know, and When Did He Know It?', in Christopher Macann, ed., *Heidegger: Critical Assessments* (London 1992), vol. 4: 377–406 – an effort that is superseded by the essay presented here.

2 In addition to the references to Zhuangzi mentioned by Reinhard May in **1.1** above, Heidegger quotes in full the story of the useless tree from the first chapter of the *Zhuangzi* in the opening section of a lecture delivered in July 1962 and published posthumously. See 'Überlieferte Sprache und technische Sprache' ('Traditional Language and Technical Language'), edited by Hermann Heidegger (Erker 1989), 7–8. Heidegger uses the Richard Wilhelm translation and refers also to the two further episodes concerning useless trees in Chapter 4. It is interesting to note that later in the lecture (p. 21) Heidegger quotes Wilhelm von Humboldt on language (a passage from *On Language*).

3 See, for example, Jacques Taminiaux, *Heidegger and the Project of Fundamental Ontology*, translated by Michael Gendre (Albany 1991).

4 See Theodore Kisiel's monumental *The Genesis of Heidegger's 'Being and Time'* (Berkeley 1993), and Theodore Kisiel and John Van Buren, eds, *Reading Heidegger from the Start* (Albany 1994).

5 'Thoughts on the Way: *Being and Time* via Lao-Chuang', in *HAT*, 105–44.

6 See *Kuki Shūzō zenshū* (*The Complete Works of Kuki Shūzō*) (Tokyo 1952), *Bekkan* (supplemental volume), 291. We learn here that in October 1922 Kuki attended Rickert's course 'From Kant to Nietzsche: Historical Introduction to Contemporary Problems', as well as two courses on Kant. The following semester he sat in on two more courses given by Rickert, 'Introduction to Epistemology and Metaphysics' and 'Philosophy of Art'.

7 See Tada Michitarō, 'Kaisetsu' (Commentary), in *'Iki' no kōzō* (Tokyo 1979), 202.

8 In a list of participants in Husserl's small seminar in the summer semester of 1922, Yama[no]uchi is named along with four other Japanese scholars, and also Karl Löwith, who would also later become a student of Heidegger (Karl Schuhmann, *Husserl-Chronik. Denk- und Lebensweg Edmund Husserls* [Den Haag 1977], 259). Yamanouchi is cited as the first Japanese to study with Heidegger by a later student, Tsujimura Kōichi, in a speech on the occasion of Heidegger's sixtieth birthday (reprinted in *JH* 159–65).

9 There are two English translations of this text: *A Study of Good*, translated by Valdo Viglielmo (Tokyo 1960), and *An Inquiry into the Good*, translated by Masao Abe and Christopher Ives (New Haven 1990). It may be fair to say that Nishida is the only major figure in Japanese philosophy of the first

half of the twentieth century *not* to have been influenced by Heidegger (perhaps in part because he was twenty years Heidegger's senior).

10 See the discussion of Yamanouchi's critique in Nishitani Keiji, *Nishida Kitarō*, translated by Yamamoto Seisaku and James W. Heisig (Berkeley 1991), 198–205.

11 A brief account of Miki's relations with Heidegger can be found in Yuasa Yasuo, 'Modern Japanese Philosophy and Heidegger', in *HAT* 155–74, 159–65.

12 See James W. Heisig, 'Foreword', in Tanabe Hajime, *Philosophy as Meta-noetics*, translated by Takeuchi Yoshinori with Valdo Viglielmo and James W. Heisig (Berkeley 1986); a translation of *Zangedō toshite no tetsugaku*, in *Tanabe Hajime zenshū* 9:3–269 (Tokyo 1972). This is the only book of Tanabe's to have been published in English translation so far, but some helpful discussions of Tanabe's ideas can be found in Taitetsu Unno and James W. Heisig, eds, *The Religious Philosophy of Tanabe Hajime: The Metanoetic Imperative* (Berkeley 1990).

13 In September 1933 Tanabe wrote a commentary on Heidegger's *Rektorats-rede*, 'The Self-Assertion of the German University', in which he mildly criticized Heidegger's 'championing [of] the racial significance of German academia'. It was published in three instalments in the *Asahi Shinbun* in October the same year, under the title 'Kiki no tetsugaku ka tetsugaku no kiki ka' ('Philosophy of Crisis or Crisis of Philosophy?'). A German translation by Elmar Weinmayr is to be found in *JH* 139–45.

14 A note in Schuhmann's *Husserl-Chronik* reads: 'SS [summer semester] 1923: Hasime [*sic*.] Tanabe nimmt an H[usserl]'s Seminar teil' (p. 269). Michiko Yusa has drawn my attention to a cordial letter from Nishida to Husserl (20 May 1925) in which Nishida gives news of both Yamanouchi and Tanabe. See Karl Schuhmann, ed., *Edmund Husserl Briefwechsel*, vol. 6 (Dordrecht 1994), 307. Volume 4 of the *Briefwechsel* contains six letters from Tanabe to Husserl written between 1922 and 1925 (pp. 509–16).

15 Heisig, 'Foreword', in *Philosophy as Metanoetics*, xi; confirmed in a conversation with Professor Yoshinori Takeuchi in June 1992.

16 See *JH* 181–8. Yuasa (in *HAT*) discusses Tanabe only briefly, and his judgement that the influence of Heidegger on Tanabe is 'relatively small' may understate the case. Tsujimura Kōichi's claim that Tanabe maintained 'a thinking dialogue with Heidegger's thought until his [Tanabe's] death in 1962' (*JH* 159) seems closer to the mark. See, for example, the references to Heidegger in *Philosophy as Metanoetics*, and also the discussion of Heidegger's influence on Tanabe by Ōhashi Ryōsuke in *JH* 25–6.

17 'Die neue Wende in der Phänomenologie – Heideggers Phänomenologie des Lebens', translated by Johannes Laube, in *JH* 89–108. Tanabe's essay first appeared in the journal *Shisō* in October 1924, and is reprinted in *Tanabe Hajime zenshū*, 4:17–34.

18 *GA* 63:114.

19 'Phänomenologische Interpretationen zu Aristoteles', edited by Hans-Ulrich Lessing, *Dilthey-Jahrbuch* 6 (1989):235–74; English translation by Michael Baur, 'Phenomenological Interpretations with respect to Aristotle', *Man and World* 25 (1992):355–93.

20 *GA* 63:31–2.

21 Martin Heidegger, *The Concept of Time*, translated by William McNeill (Oxford 1992), 11–13 and 21. See also the *Prolegomena zur Geschichte des Zeitbegriffs* of 1925 (*GA* 20:403), where the nothingness of *die Welt* is related, by way of the revelatory phenomenon of *Angst*, to the absolute nothingness of death in a way that prefigures the fuller treatment in *Being and Time* (§§ 49, 53, 57, 68b).

110   *Complementary essay*

22 'Phänomenologische Interpretationen zu Aristoteles', 244; 'Phenomenological Interpretations', 365 (translation modified).
23 'Anmerkungen zu Karl Jaspers *Psychologie der Weltanschauungen*', in *Wm*,
GA 9:1–44. For an account of Heidegger's debt to Georg Simmel, in the
context of an illuminating discussion of the problematic of death in *Being
and Time*, see David Farrell Krell, *Daimon Life: Heidegger and Life-
Philosophy* (Bloomington 1992), Chapter 2.
24 'Anmerkungen zu Karl Jaspers', *GA* 9:25–6. (There is a minor misprint in
the second sentence quoted from Jaspers, where Heidegger's text has
'Zugrundegehen des einen Wesens' instead of 'des eigenen Wesens' for 'of
one's own being'.)
25 In his footnote Heidegger emphasizes, in turn, pp. 259–70 of the third edition
(Berlin 1925) of *Psychologie der Weltanschauungen*, though the citations in
the 'Anmerkungen' were, naturally, to the first edition. Subsequent references to this text in the present essay will be to the third edition.
26 Tanabe Hajime, 'Todesdialektik', in *Martin Heidegger zum siebzigsten
Geburtstag: Festschrift* (Pfullingen 1959), 93–133.
27 According to the Japanologist Wolfram Naumann, Heidegger and Tanabe
'regarded one another as mutually giving and receiving partners in a commu-
nity of thinking' ('Japan als Gegenstand der Forschung', in *Einsichten.
Forschung an der Ludwig-Maximilians-Universität München* [1995], 1:32–5,
34).
28 Otto Pöggeler, *Martin Heidegger's Path of Thinking*, translated by Daniel
Magurshak and Sigmund Barber (Atlantic Highlands 1987), Chapter 2.
29 John Van Buren, 'Martin Heidegger, Martin Luther,' in Kisiel and Van Buren,
eds, *Reading Heidegger from the Start*, 159–74.
30 Augustine, *De civitate dei*, 13.10. See the careful elucidation of this point,
and of the parallel with Heidegger, in Johann Kreuzer, *Pulchritudo. Vom
Erkennen Gottes bei Augustin* (Munich 1995), 176ff. John Van Buren notes
that a loose page that has been published with Heidegger's first Aristotle
course from the end of 1921 (*GA* 61:182) contains a quotation from Luther's
Commentary on Genesis in which he calls life a constant *cursus ad mortem*
('Martin Heidegger, Martin Luther', 171).
31 A significant anticipation of the role of death in Heidegger's analysis of
Dasein is to be found in an earlier phenomenology – in Hegel's account of
the role of death in the attainment of freedom of self-consciousness in *The
Phenomenology of Spirit*. We read in the preface that it is only by refusing
to shy away from 'the monstrous power of the negative ... Death ... the
most terrible' that the life of spirit comes fully into its own: 'It attains its
truth only insofar as it finds itself in absolute dismemberment [*Zerrissenheit*]'.
The life of spirit must allow itself to be torn away from 'natural life', in order
to 'bear death and preserve itself in death' (Hegel, *Phänomenologie des
Geistes* [Hamburg 1952], 29–30; *Hegel's Phenomenology of Spirit*, translated
by A. V. Miller [Oxford 1977], 19 [§ 32] – translation modified). See also the
later discussion of death in the section 'Absolute Freedom and Terror', where
the negation of the self in absolute freedom comes about by 'meaningless
death, the pure terror of the negative' – but where this negation may, as
'universal will', be transformed into its opposite: 'and meaningless death, the
unfulfilled negativity of the self, turns in the inner concept into absolute posi-
tivity'.
    In the struggle between Master and Slave, each can attain the freedom of
self-consciousness only through an engagement with death. The account of
the slavish consciousness' attainment of self-consciousness vividly prefigures

some of the corresponding language in *Being and Time*: 'For this consciousness has had anxiety [*Angst*] not over this or that, nor for this moment [*Augenblick*] or that, but for its entire being; for it has felt the fear of death, the absolute master. It has thereby been subject to an inner dissolution, has trembled throughout its being, and everything stable within it has been shaken' (B.IV.A).

32 Heidegger uses this phrase in discussing the letters of the Apostle Paul in his lecture course 'Einführung in die Phänomenologie der Religion' (Freiburg, winter semester 1920–1); referred to by Pöggeler, *Martin Heidegger's Path of Thinking*, Chapter 2.

33 Though *Philosophy as Metanoetics* was not published until 1946, the manuscript had been completed in 1944.

34 *Tanabe Hajime zenshū*, 9:397ff, esp. 474. See James Heisig, 'The "Self That is Not a Self"', in Unno and Heisig, eds, *The Religious Philosophy of Tanabe Hajime*, 288 (where a misprint gives the pages of the Tanabe passage as 190ff). Heisig mentions the influence of Heidegger here, but suggests that 'Heidegger could not have [related the practice of death to] the story of Jesus and the Zen samurai ideal'. In the light of the considerations contained in the present volume, one might be tempted to say that perhaps Heidegger could have, after all.

35 This essay is available in an English translation by Valdo Viglielmo in *Philosophical Studies of Japan* 1 (1959):1–12.

36 Tanabe Hajime, 'Memento Mori', 3. Heidegger cites a passage from one of Rilke's letters from Muzot which emphasizes that the *Duino Elegies* are concerned with the essential unity of the affirmation of life and of death: 'Death is the *side of life* that is turned away from us, unillumined by us: we must try to achieve the greatest awareness of our Dasein, which is at home in *both inseparable realms, inexhaustibly nourished from both* ...' (Rainer Maria Rilke, *Briefe* [Frankfurt 1950], 896). Heidegger quotes only the first clause of this sentence – which is strange, since the second part seems to offer a more appropriate basis for the commentary which follows: 'Death and the realm of the dead belong to the totality of beings as its other side' ('What Are Poets For?', in *PLT* 124/*Hw* 279).

37 *Tanabe Hajime zenshū*, 13:525–80.

38 Ōhashi Ryōsuke, 'Die frühe Heidegger-Rezeption in Japan', in *JH* 23–37, 26. Ōhashi is surely right to suggest that Tanabe's 1924 essay on Heidegger, when read in the light of Tanabe's later writings on the topic of death, can be seen as the first step in his 'negative' Heidegger-reception.

39 See Hans Waldenfels, *Absolute Nothingness*, translated by J. W. Heisig (New York 1980), 37–9. Nishida practised Zen meditation regularly from around 1896 to 1908 or so. Though he wrote most of the manuscript of *An Inquiry into the Good* during the last few years of this period, he had apparently given up formal sitting by the time of its publication in 1911, when the development of his own philosophy was well under way. The characterization of Nishida's enterprise as the attempt to work out a new philosophy of Zen Buddhism in Western philosophical terms may be overly simple but it is not entirely misleading. (See also above, **3.1.2.**)

40 See Nishitani, *Nishida Kitarō*, Chapter 9, 'The Philosophy of Nishida and Tanabe'.

41 Nishida, *An Inquiry into the Good*, Chapter 14 (James Heisig's translation in *Absolute Nothingness*, 40–1).

42 *An Inquiry into the Good*, Chapter 31 (Heisig translation, p. 41). Nishida's understanding of God, conditioned as it is by the Buddhist idea of *mu*, is one Heidegger would not have found uncongenial.

43   Nishida Kitarō, *Intuition and Reflection in Self-Consciousness*, translated by Valdo H. Viglielmo with Takeuchi Yoshinori and Joseph S. O'Leary (Albany 1987), 140–1; a translation of *Jikaku ni okeru chokkan to hansei*, in *Nishida Kitarō zenshū*, vol. 2 (Tokyo 1978). (Heidegger's attention may have been drawn to this work, if not by Tanabe, then by Kuki Shūzō, who refers to it in a lecture he gave shortly after his sojourn in Marburg: see '*Propos* on Japan', in Stephen Light, *Shūzō Kuki and Jean-Paul Sartre* [Carbondale 1987 – hereafter *KS*], 72, which also contains translations of some of Kuki's brief essays from the period just before he met Heidegger.) In the previous section Nishida cites Max Stirner's *The Ego and its Own*, and adds: 'No concept can capture and no quality can exhaust the self, which comes from, and returns to, creative nothingness' (p. 134). For a discussion of the remarkable parallels between this idea of Stirner's and late Buddhist conceptions of nothingness, see Nishitani Keiji, *The Self-Overcoming of Nihilism*, translated by Graham Parkes with Setsuko Aihara (Albany 1990), Chapter 6.

44   For Nishida's familiarity with the *Laozi* and *Zhuangzi*, see Lothar Knauth, 'Life is Tragic – The Diary of Nishida Kitarō', *Monumenta Nipponica* 20 (1967):335–8, 349, referring to entries from the end of 1897. For a fuller account of Nishida's youth, see Valdo Humbert Viglielmo, 'Nishida Kitarō: The Early Years', in Donald H. Shively, ed., *Tradition and Modernization in Japanese Culture* (Princeton 1971).

45   *Nishida Kitarō zenshū*, 3:133, 141. I am grateful to my colleague Valdo Viglielmo for showing me draft translations of this essay and of the essays in *Hataraku mono kara miru mono e*, done by him and David Dilworth.

46   See, for example, *Nishida Kitarō zenshū*, 4:155, 207, 213, 218, 224–5, 38ff.

47   For an insightful comparison of aspects of Nishida's philosophy with Heidegger's thought, see Elmar Weinmayr, 'Denken im Übergang – Kitarō Nishida und Martin Heidegger', in *JH* 39–61. While Weinmayr is not concerned with the question of influence (though he writes at one point that 'direct influence appears to be ruled out'), some of the parallels he draws are striking. Near the beginning, for example, he juxtaposes these two passages, the first from Heidegger's Nietzsche lectures during the mid-1930s, and the second from an essay by Nishida from 1924:
   'We think that an entity is accessible by virtue of an I as subject's representing [to itself] an object. As if beforehand there would not be the necessity for an Open to prevail, within whose openness something ... can become accessible *as* object *for* a subject!' (*Nietzsche* 2:138).
   'In order for consciousness and the object to be able to relate to one another, there must be something that includes both within it. There must be something like a place in which the two can relate to one another' (*Nishida Kitarō zenshū*, 4:211).

48   Aihara Shinsaku, 'Tanabe-sensei ni tsuite' ('On Professor Tanabe'), in *Tanabe tetsugaku* (*Tanabe's philosophy*) (Tokyo 1951), 264.

49   Conversation at Professor Takeuchi's home in Yokkaichi, June 1992.

50   Conversation with Professor Tsujimura in Kyoto, June 1992. Ernst Friedrich Ferdinand Zermelo (1871–1953), a friend of Husserl's, was famous for his contributions to axiomatic set theory – a subject that interested Tanabe throughout his career.

51   *WL* 37/*US* 131. The Inquirer says earlier (3/87) that he often discussed this question with Kuki Shūzō.

52   Hegel, *Wissenschaft der Logik*, Book I, section 1, Chapter 1, C. *Werden*, 1. 'Einheit des Seins und Nichts', and *Anmerkung* 1.

53   Quoted by Reinhard May above, **3.1.3**.

54 Max Scheler, 'Vom Wesen der Philosophie', in *Vom Ewigen im Menschen*, in *Gesammelte Werke* (Bern 1954), 5:93.

55 Max Scheler, 'Probleme der Religion', in *Vom Ewigen im Menschen*, 263–4.

56 Personal communication from Otto Pöggeler, September 1991.

57 *Zen: Der lebendige Buddhismus in Japan, Ausgewählte Stücke des Zen-Textes*, übersetzt und eingeleitet von Schüej Ōhasama, herausgegeben von August Faust, mit einem Geleitwort von Rudolf Otto (Gotha/Stuttgart 1925). See above, **3.1.2**. For Nishitani Keiji's report that Heidegger had taken this book out of the Freiburg University library and found it 'very interesting', see my introduction to *HAT* (p. 10).

58 In talking about the many Japanese scholars who came to Heidelberg to study with Heinrich Rickert, Hermann Glockner mentions that August Faust was obliged to become an early riser during his sojourn in Freiburg (in 1922) thanks to his enthusiasm for Heidegger's classes (*Heidelberger Bilderbuch. Erinnerungen von Hermann Glockner* [Bonn 1969], 197). Glockner paints an interesting picture of Ōhazama Shūei too (227–43), and also gives a brief account of Kuki's studying with Rickert (232).

59 *Zen: Der lebendige Buddhismus in Japan*, 63. The verse from Hakuin that stands as the epigraph to Ōhazama's foreword prefigures Heidegger's later talk of Being as 'nearness' or *das Nächste*: 'Woe to those who seek in the far distance [*in weiter Ferne*] / and ignore what lies near [*nahe*]!' (p. xiv).

60 Ōhazama distinguishes consummate nothingness from 'empty, abstract noth-ingness' in terms that prefigure Heidegger's discussions in works from the late 1920s and early 1930s: 'Consummate nothingness is not to be found through abstracting negation but through the concentration of everything concrete. It is thus not empty, but full through and through. It is the absolute, the totality standing over all parts, the perfection standing over all oppo-sites, the freedom [*Freiheit*] standing over all causal contexts. It is the highest truth [*Wahrheit*] itself' (pp. 134–5). It is also the 'twenty-first nothingness' – 'the consummate nothingness of not-nothingness' (148–9).

61 See Miki's letter of 19 June 1924, in *Miki Kiyoshi zenshū*, 19: 277–8. My thanks to Michiko Yusa for providing this reference.

62 *Martin Heidegger/Karl Jaspers: Briefwechsel, 1920–1963*, edited by Walter Biemel and Hans Saner (Frankfurt 1990), 48.

63 The entry for 12 October 1927 in the *Husserl-Chronik* reads: 'The evening [at Husserl's home] was very nice, nothing but philosophers . . . and the most interesting couple: the Kukis'. Roman Ingarden, who was there that evening, reports that 'Heidegger came from Marburg for just a short visit' (p. 325). Kuki subsequently went back to Paris, and it was then that he came to know the young Jean-Paul Sartre: see Light, *Shūzō Kuki and Jean-Paul Sartre*.

64 *Kuki Shūzō zenshū*, Bekkan, 293. In Freiburg Kuki attended Heidegger's course on Kant's first critique and his seminar on Schelling's *Treatise on the Nature of Human Freedom*; in Marburg he audited Heidegger's course on Leibniz and his seminar on Aristotle's *Physics*.

65 See Ōhashi Ryōsuke, in *JH* 29.

66 Stephen Light cites a report to the effect that in 1957 Heidegger expressed (to Tsujimura Kōichi) his desire to write a preface to an anticipated German translation of one of Kuki's books (*KS* 31, note 16) – a significant desire when one considers that by that time Heidegger can hardly have been casting around for books for which to write prefaces.

67 The kind of evidence one would hope would be available – diaries from the period by Kuki or his wife, letters sent to friends in Japan – is unfortunately lacking, according to the staff responsible for the Kuki archive at Kōnan University.

68 Ōhashi Ryōsuke, 'Heidegger und Graf Kuki: Zu Sprache und Kunst in Japan als Problem der Moderne', in H.-H. Gander, ed., *Von Heidegger her: Messkircher Vorträge 1989* (Frankfurt a. M. 1991), 93–104, 96. Ōhashi also points out three errors in the picture of Kuki that emerges from Heidegger's 'Conversation': the correct equivalent for Kuki's title would be 'Baron' rather than 'Count'; while the 'Japanese' says that Nishida was Kuki's teacher, the latter had gone to Tokyo University rather than Kyoto and did not become a colleague of Nishida's at Kyoto until 1935; nor is it the case, as Heidegger's 'Japanese' says, that Kuki's lectures at Kyoto on 'the aesthetics of Japanese art and poetry . . . appeared as a book' (94).

69 '*Iki* may therefore be thought of as a remarkable self-expression of specific modes of existence in oriental cultures, or more narrowly in the Yamato [ancient Japanese] people' (*Kuki Shūzō zenshū*, 1:1–86, 12). References to '*Iki' no kōzō* will be made by the abbreviation *IK* followed by the page number of this edition.

70 This moment of *iki* as possibility is said to 'naturally disappear if the sexes achieve union and thereby lose the tension' (*IK* 17). Whereas Kuki emphasizes the preservation of possibility with respect to sex, Heidegger does so with respect to death (*SZ* § 53).

71 For a brief discussion of this maxim, see the section 'The Way of the Sword' in my 'Japanese Ways of Thinking', in Robert Solomon, ed., *From Africa to Zen: An Introduction to World Philosophy* (Savage, Md. 1992), 25–53.

72 The texts of these lectures were published as a book, *Propos sur le temps*, in Paris in 1928; English translations can be found in *KS* 43–67.

73 Light, *Shūzō Kuki and Jean-Paul Sartre*, 43. Kuki's mention of Heidegger's theory of temporality at the beginning of the first talk constitutes one of the earliest introductions of Heidegger's ideas in France – the discussion of which would later become a major industry.

74 Heidegger, *SZ* 384–5. The similarity with Zen ideas puts Tanabe's criticism of Heidegger for emphasizing 'self-power' at the expense of 'other-power' in a different light. It is a salient feature of Heidegger's elaboration of the authentic response to the confrontation with death that one is acutely aware of one's 'powerlessness' (*Ohnmacht*) in the situation, and that once the '*Man-selbst*' has shattered itself through the confrontation with death, one is then able to let the 'authentic self' – definitely something Other – 'operate through one' (*in-sich-handeln-lassen*). Heidegger writes that in understanding the call of conscience, Dasein 'lets the ownmost self *operate through it*' (*SZ* 288), and speaks later, in the same context, of the 'letting the ownmost self operate through it' (*SZ* 295). These ideas bear a remarkable similarity to the Zen idea that if one effects a full confrontation with death, then 'Great Life', 'No-mind', or the 'True Self' will work and play through the field of one's body.

75 Incidentally, a contemporary Japanese philosopher claims that the earliest use of the term *In-der-Welt-sein*, resplendent with hyphens, occurs not in *Being and Time* but in a German translation of Okakura's *The Book of Tea* that was published in 1919 (Imamichi Tomonobu, *Betrachtungen über das Eine* [Tokyo 1968], 154). Okakura uses the term with reference to Daoism, which he calls 'the art of being in the world' (see the chapter 'Taoism and Zennism' in *The Book of Tea*).

76 Petzet, 168–70/177–9.

77 The discussion in the dialogue with the Japanese about the pregnant gestures of Noh drama, where the Japanese demonstrates a gesture evoking a mountain landscape (*WL* 18/*US* 107), echoes a line in Kuki's *Propos* concerning Japanese theatre: 'Hands shading the eyes will make one think of a moun-

tain landscape' (*KS* 75 – where Kuki is actually quoting from a French commentary: Albert Maybon, *Le théâtre japonais* [Paris 1925]).

78 See Michiko Yoneda, *Gespräch und Dichtung*, 88–96, who reports (p. 91) Tezuka's saying that he did not know Kuki personally or attend his lectures, and that he was actually not very conversant with Heidegger's writings – so that he could not possibly have uttered many of the things ascribed to the visitor from Japan.

79 See Reinhard May above, **1.1** and **3.2.1**.

80 Rudolf Otto, 'Meister Eckeharts Mystik im Unterschiede von östlicher Mystik', *Zeitschrift für Theologie und Kirche* (1925), 325–50 and 418–36. In a footnote in his *Habilitationsschrift* of 1916, Heidegger evinces a desire to write a philosophical appraisal of Eckhart's mysticism (*Frühe Schriften*, 344).

81 Rudolf Otto, 'Der östliche Buddhist', *Die Christliche Welt* (1925), 978–82.

82 In the foreword to *Frühe Schriften* (p. x; *GA* 1:56), Heidegger writes: 'In the seminar exercises with Rickert I became acquainted with the writings of Emil Lask, who, mediating between [Rickert and Husserl], also tried to attend to the Greek thinkers'.

83 It is ironical that while Heidegger protested 'the nihilistic misinterpretation' (prevalent in Europe) of his idea of nothingness, Tanabe eventually came to level a similar criticism at Heidegger. Johannes Laube notes that Tanabe's copy of the 1948 edition of *Was ist Metaphysik?* contains marginalia in Tanabe's hand that become ever more critical, from page to page, of Heidegger's conception of *Nichts* as a mere negation of being and *nihilistisches Nichts*. See Naumann, 'Japan als Gegenstand der Forschung', 34.

84 Kojima wrote a long letter to Heidegger in 1963 which was subsequently published together with a lengthy reply as a pair of 'open letters' in both Japanese and German. Kojima starts out by saying that when an outline of Heidegger's *Gelassenheit* was published in a Japanese newspaper, 'it almost seemed to us as if you, Herr Professor, were directly addressing us Japanese' (*JH* 216). This impression is no grounds for amazement, in view of the allusions in that text to both Zen and Daoism; see the excerpt from Kojima's letter quoted and discussed in **3.1.1** above.

85 It is also around this time, in the mid-1930s, that Heidegger turns his attention to the poetry of Hölderlin – the first of several German poets whose work will inspire his philosophical thinking. Later, in the 'Letter on Humanism', he writes (though presumably alluding to what was called 'the Near East' rather than to the Far East): 'We have hardly begun to think the mysterious relations to the East that have been given voice in Hölderlin's poetry' (*Wm* 169). See Otto Pöggeler's discussion of Heidegger's interest in the poets in the light of his acquaintance with Daoism (*HAT* 62–8).

86 *An Introduction to Metaphysics*, 26/20. Heidegger's keen interest in Bashō is attested by Tezuka Tomio (see above, **2.2.1** and Chapter 7; also note 98 below) and Tsujimura Kōichi (*JH* 265). See also the discussion of Bashō in a Heideggerian context in Yoneda, *Gespräch und Dichtung*, 186–225.

87 *An Introduction to Metaphysics*, 76, 38, 57/58, 29, 43. For further discussion of this topic, see my essay, 'From Nationalism to Nomadism: Wondering about the Languages of Philosophy', in Eliot Deutsch, ed., *Culture and Modernity: East and West* (Honolulu 1991), 455–67.

88 Graham Parkes, 'Thoughts on the Way: *Being and Time* via Lao-Chuang', in *HAT* 105–44, especially the 'Epilogue'. Footnote 9 of that essay stands in need of revision: as Reinhard May has pointed out, the Buber edition of the *Zhuangzi* was first published in 1910, not 1921, and so there was ample time for Heidegger to discover the text and assimilate its ideas by the time he wrote his works of the mid-1930s.

89 See the diagram and dialogue in 'Thoughts on the Way,' *HAT* 137. Compare Richard Wilhelm, *I Ging: Das Buch der Wandlungen* (Düsseldorf 1970), 14–16, 25, 30, 272–6. The assumption that Heidegger had read the *I jing* is not necessary: he could have gleaned an adequate sense of ideas such as *yin* and *yang* from his conversations with Kuki and/or readings of the other Daoist classics and the commentaries of the translators or editors.

90 Elmar Weinmayr refers to this passage about the *offene Mitte* in explicating Nishida's idea of 'the place of absolute nothing' as 'the place of arising and perishing' (*JH* 44). This place, which Nishida explicated at length in the mid-1920s, is indeed reminiscent of Heidegger's clearing, 'into which all that is stands and from which it withdraws itself' (*PLT* 52/*Hw* 41).

91 Nishida uses the verb *urazukeru*, 'to be lined', as in a passage from *Hataraku mono kara miru mono e* (*From acting to seeing*) where he writes of nothingness as 'the inner *lining* of being' (*Nishida Kitarō zenshū*, 4:227). See also the entry under 'lining' in the glossary of Robert Schinzinger's translation of *Kitarō Nishida: Intelligibility and the Philosophy of Nothingness* (Honolulu 1966), which includes a translation of the 1928 essay 'Eichiteki sekai' ('The Intelligible World') where this term occurs again.

92 D. T. Suzuki, 'Erinnerung an einen Besuch bei Martin Heidegger', in *JH* 169–72.

93 Personal communication from Michiko Yusa, November 1995. Takahashi Fumi was the translator of the essay by Nishida (referred to by Reinhard May in **3.1.2** above) that was published in German in 1939 in the *Proceedings* of the Prussian Academy of Sciences in Berlin.

94 *GA*, 5:70–4; editor's note, 377. My thanks to Holger Krüger (Düsseldorf/Essen) for adducing the following quote from the *Zusatz*.

95 *WL* 8, 24/*US* 94, 115, to be discussed in the following section.

96 Two of Nishitani's works containing some discussion of Heidegger have been translated: *Religion and Nothingness*, translated by Jan Van Bragt (Berkeley 1982), and *The Self-Overcoming of Nihilism*, translated by Graham Parkes with Setsuko Aihara (Albany 1990). This latter text devotes an entire chapter to Heidegger's thought, although – written a dozen or so years earlier than *Religion and Nothingness* – the Heidegger in it appears comparatively 'undigested'.

97 See my introduction to *HAT*, 9–10.

98 In an appendix to the Japanese translation of 'Aus einem Gespräch von der Sprache', Tezuka Tomio recalls how during his meeting with Heidegger in 1954, the latter brought the conversation around to a *haiku* by Bashō he had read in translation: 'He asked me about the poem in Japanese and posed a number of perspicacious questions about the special nature of Japanese thought as it manifests in language and in art. During my rather inept explanations it seemed as if various thoughts occurred in rapid succession to this prominent thinker. He took notes with great zeal' (*JH* 179).

99 Nishitani Keiji, 'Gendai bunmei ni fukai kikikan', *Yomiuri Shinbun* 27 May 1976; translated by Elmar Weinmayr as 'Ein tiefes Gefühl für die Krise der modernen Zivilisation', in *JH* 193–4.

100 *Martin Heidegger/Karl Jaspers: Briefwechsel*, 178, 280.

101 It is worth noting with respect to Heidegger's expression of scepticism concerning 'Eastern thinking' in this passage that the Greek roots of the term *skeptisch* (*skepsis, skeptomai*) have to do, as he well knew, with 'examining closely'. In this sense he would seem to be admitting that with the unfamiliar language of Chinese he is concerned to 'examine closely'.

102 Although most of the passages from Heidegger in this section have been discussed above by Reinhard May, they appear in a different light in the

context of this complementary essay. For the 'Conversation' as 'confession', see Chapter 5 above.

103 *Identität und Differenz* (Pfullingen 1957), 25; *Identity and Difference* (New York 1969), 36.

104 See Paul Shih-yi Hsiao, 'Heidegger and Our Translation of the *Tao Te Ching*', in *HAT* 93–104. This translation work was kept secret until after Heidegger's death: see above, **1.2.2**, note 23. This secrecy may account for the fact – strange in view of how much of Heidegger's *Nachlass* has been preserved – that no written record of his summer's work with Professor Hsiao has been found.

105 See Reinhard May above, **1.1**.

106 *Vorträge und Aufsätze* (Pfullingen 1967), I, 39; 'Science and Reflection', in *The Question concerning Technology and Other Essays*, translated by William Lovitt (New York 1977), 158.

107 *WL* 24/*US*, 115. For an intelligent discussion of the relations between Heidegger's philosophy and Japanese thinking, with special attention to his conceptions of metaphysics and technology, the issue of intercultural understanding, and considerations of translation between Japanese and Indo-European languages, see section 4 of Elmar Weinmayr, *Entstellung: Die Metaphysik im Denken Martin Heideggers, mit einem Blick nach Japan* (Munich 1991), 271–312.

108 'Hölderlins Erde und Himmel', *Hölderlin-Jahrbuch* 11 (1958–60), 36; quoted above, **5.2**.

109 'Nur noch ein Gott kann uns retten', *Der Spiegel* 30/23 (May 1976), reprinted in G. Neske, ed., *Antwort: Martin Heidegger im Gespräch* (Pfullingen 1988), 106.

110 D. T. Suzuki, *Zen Buddhism*, edited by William Barrett (New York 1956), xi–xii. One is less inclined to dismiss this report as being purely apocryphal in the light of Petzet's report (mentioned in **1.1** above) to the effect that Heidegger responded to the Buddhist monk from Thailand's characterization of 'nothingness' as 'fullness' with the words: 'That is what I have been saying, my whole life long' (P 180/190).

111 *Kōza-Zen* 8 (Tokyo 1968), 321f; reprinted in *JH* 230–1.

112 Hans A. Fischer-Barnicol reports that Heidegger once said to him, after remarking that from early on he had worked with Japanese philosophers, that 'he had nevertheless learned more from the Chinese' (see above, **1.2.3**). This is a telling remark: in so far as none of Heidegger's Chinese visitors came close, as philosophers, to the calibre of Tanabe, Miki, Kuki, or Nishitani, one should perhaps take *von den Chinesen* to refer to the classical Chinese thinkers he had read in German translation.

Index